WORLD
RACECOURSES

Published by Collins
An imprint of HarperCollins Publishers
Westerhill Road
Bishopbriggs
Glasgow G64 2QT

www.harpercollins.co.uk

First edition 2018

A catalogue record for this book is available from the British Library.

ISBN 978-0-00-828497-8

10 9 8 7 6 5 4 3 2 1

Printed in China

If you would like to comment on any aspect of this book, please contact us at the above address or online.
email: collins.reference@harpercollins.co.uk

  facebook.com/collinsref

@collins_ref

WORLD RACECOURSES

CORNELIUS LYSAGHT

FOREWORD BY *Frankie Dettori*

Contents

Foreword

Every racecourse plays a part in the story of horseracing and I am delighted that Cornelius Lysaght has gathered together one hundred of the most significant, historic and unusual tracks, and told their tales. These places illustrate the fascinating history of racing and of its colourful and vibrant presence throughout the world. Their locations may vary from the rolling downs to the busy city to the desert, but they are all connected by two things: a love of racehorses and a desire to show them at their best. These are captured superbly in the stunning photographs throughout the book.

Since my first success in Turin in November 1986, I have had the privilege of competing at many of the courses featured, and a whole lot of them hold a very special place in my heart, particularly, of course, Ascot, which provided the setting for one of the highlights of my career, the 'Magnificent Seven' of 1996 - when I was lucky enough to win all seven races on the card - and also Newmarket where I was so pleased to reach the milestone of 3,000 winners, in 2016.

Each arena has its own individual style and charm, thereby creating the great variety of venues for which racing around the globe is renowned. Who could fail to be impressed by the elegance of Chantilly in France, or the skyscraper-surrounded Happy Valley in Hong Kong, or the tradition and ceremony of Royal Ascot, or the sheer uniqueness of the 'White Turf' at St Moritz in Switzerland?

Naturally, the histories of these racecourses would not be complete without all of the horses, the owners, trainers and jockeys and the many others who have made their mark at them, and I have very much enjoyed reading the intriguing array of connected stories too. I hope you do as well.

Frankie Dettori MBE

Picture opposite: *Another victorious flying dismount from Frankie Dettori after Without Parole's success at Royal Ascot, 2018*

Introduction

I've always thought that there are three factors that attract people to horseracing in the first place: naturally, one is a fascination with the animal itself and its physical make-up; then, there is the fascination with the gambling that has galloped alongside the sport practically since the beginning of time; and the third is a fascination with the 'world' of racing.

Being from a relatively non-horsy background and too challenged on the pecuniary front to be recklessly risk-averse, my introduction came mainly under the latter banner: a fascination with the horses, yes, but in combination with the people involved with them and the stages on which they all perform.

I have no specific recollection of the curtain going up on my own racing world, though it was in the Welsh Borders at Hereford during my childhood growing up in the area that I was taken to the races for the first time. On all-too-occasional visits to the course now, in my capacity as the BBC's racing correspondent, my mind is sent spiralling back to those carefree days of following the action, with the city sprawling all around and the Black Mountains in the distance.

Sadly, to mix my sporting metaphors badly, Hereford did not make the cut this time, but racing's variety of locations, whether they be semi-rural like that one, or 'middle-of-nowhere' or urban is one of its most enduring attractions and in this book I seek to cover a bit of everything.

When Collins came up with the idea for the project, the principal concern was an embarrassment of riches – there are something like 325 courses in Britain, Ireland and France alone, and we had, I was told, room for just 100 from around the globe.

The greatest tracks on all continents are featured, many of them dripping with character and heritage: places like Ascot, Cheltenham and the rebranded ParisLongchamp in Europe; in North America, Churchill Downs and Santa Anita; San Isidro in Buenos Aires, South America; Meydan and Tokyo in Asia; and Oceania's number one, Flemington in Melbourne.

But I also wanted to highlight the simply spectacular, from Laytown and its beach to St Moritz and its snow to Del Mar and its glitz to Gávea and its monument to Kenilworth and its nature reserve to Birdsville and its sand. Plus, of course, all points in between.

They are ordered from continent to continent, starting in Europe and continuing on something of a roller coaster ride around the world, ending up in Oceania; within each section, the courses are listed in countries, which are themselves in alphabetical order.

Although different people refer to different tracks in different ways, I concluded the simplest thing was to stick, where there was any debate, with location as opposed to the name of the arena. Hence Cheltenham rather than Prestbury Park, Santiago not Club Hípico.

I am so pleased and grateful to Frankie Dettori, for the foreword. As well as being the most brilliant of horsemen and the greatest of showmen, on whom all racing journalists have been fortunate enough to report for literally decades, he is also truly an international jockey – and not just for being Italian-born, but British-based – and his trademark flying dismount has been witnessed at many of the courses contained within these pages. There could hardly be a more appropriate writer.

Thanks too to Dan Abraham for masterminding his network of contacts to source the pictures; to a long list of those that have helped, but particularly Michael Andrews, Tim Cox, Sean Magee and Ed Prosser; to the late and much-missed George Ennor for his invaluable *World Encyclopedia of Horse Racing*, compiled with Bill Mooney and published by Carlton Books in 2001, into which I take an almost daily dip; and to Jethro Lennox, Sarah Woods, Karen Midgley and the rest of the team at the Collins stable.

I hope that you enjoy reading it all as much as I have enjoyed compiling it.
Good luck, and thank you.

Cornelius Lysaght
South Warwickshire, June 2018

Racecourse Locator Map

NORTH AMERICA

Hastings Park

Arlington

Woodbine

Saratoga

Santa Anita Park

Churchill Downs

Belmont Park

Del Mar

Keeneland

Pimlico

Gulfstream Park

Mexico City

Canóvanas

Martinique

Garrison Savannah

Caracas

Santa Rosa Park

Panama City

Guayaquil

SOUTH AMERICA

Monterrico

Cidade Jardim

Gávea

Asunción

Santiago

Montevideo

San Isidro

EUROPE

Øvrevoll

Bro Park

Casablanca-Anfa

AFRICA

Kenilworth

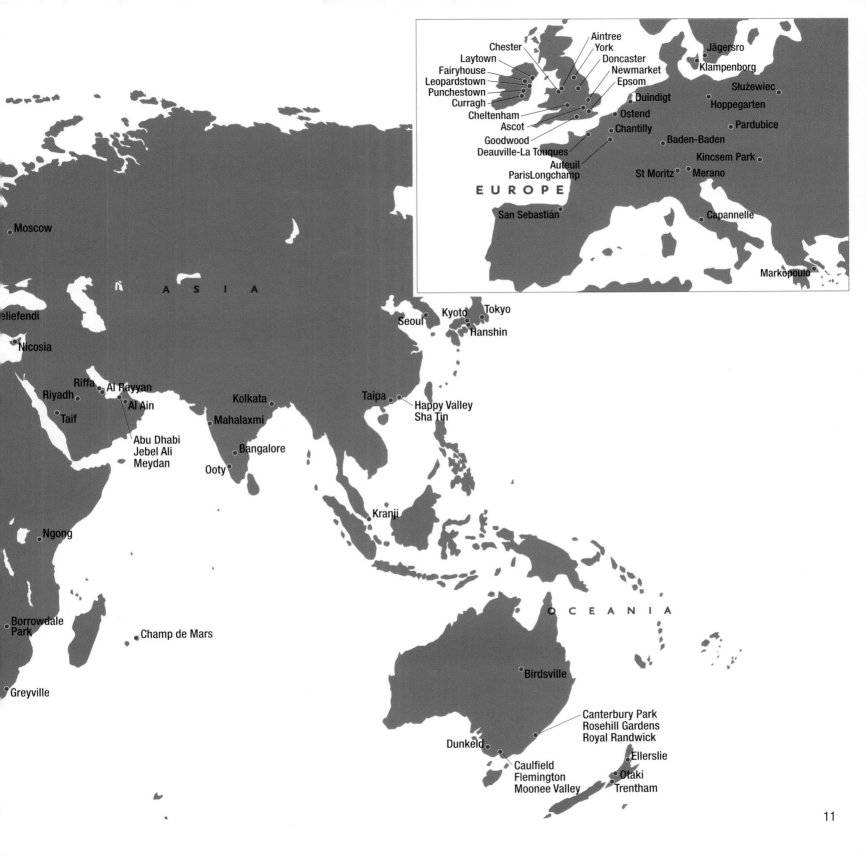

Moscow

eliefendi

Nicosia

Riffa · Al Rayyan
Riyadh ·
Taif · · Al Ain

Abu Dhabi
Jebel Ali
Meydan

Kolkata
Mahalaxmi

Bangalore

Ooty

Ngong

Borrowdale
Park

Champ de Mars

Greyville

ASIA

Seoul · Kyoto · Tokyo
Hanshin

Taipa · Happy Valley
Sha Tin

Kranji

OCEANIA

Birdsville

Dunkeld

Caulfield
Flemington
Moonee Valley

Canterbury Park
Rosehill Gardens
Royal Randwick

Ellerslie

Otaki
Trentham

EUROPE

Chester
Laytown
Fairyhouse
Leopardstown
Punchestown
Curragh
Cheltenham
Ascot
Goodwood
Deauville-La Touques
Auteuil
ParisLongchamp

Aintree
York
Doncaster
Newmarket
Epsom
Duindigt
Ostend
Chantilly

Jägersro
Klampenborg
Służewiec
Hoppegarten
Pardubice
Baden-Baden
Kincsem Park
St Moritz · Merano

San Sebastián

Capannelle

Markopoulo

11

Europe

Ostend

Belgium

LOCATION: ADJACENT TO THE BEACH IN THE HEART OF THE BELGIAN COASTAL CITY

THE TRACK: RIGHT-HANDED, OVAL, TURF, AROUND A MILE (1,600M) WITH A STRAIGHT SPRINT COURSE; HOLDS MEETINGS BETWEEN JULY AND AUGUST

PRINCIPAL RACES: PRIX PRINCE ROSE, JULY

OPENED: 1883

FAMOUS MOMENTS: BELGIAN HERO PRINCE ROSE BEATS THE BRILLIANT FRENCH MARE PEARL CAP IN THE 1931 GRAND INTERNATIONAL D'OSTENDE

Some racecourses are sadly serving only as monuments to the past, but it must be hoped that the renaissance of the grand old track of Ostend will continue long into the future. It is named the Wellington Renbaan, after the Duke of Wellington, who fought there in the 1794 Flanders Campaign before later defeating Napoleon at Waterloo. The neo-classical grandstand backs onto the beach and was built on the site of a Napoleonic fort.

The course was a popular destination during much of the twentieth century before its fortunes dwindled, and it even lay dormant for four years from 2008. Happily, it has re-emerged with summer fixtures proving a hit with holidaymakers, and even attracting a full house of 9,500 on one occasion.

There are various Flat races on a tight circuit, which surrounds a golf course, usually between local horses and moderate French rivals. The biggest race is the Prix Prince Rose, formerly known as the Grand International d'Ostende but now named after Belgium's greatest horse. It used to be a significant prize, won by future Prix de l'Arc de Triomphe winner Rheingold (1973) and Arc runner-up Argument (1980). Nowadays it is just a middle-tier handicap.

Pardubice

Czechia

LOCATION: IN THE CITY OF PARDUBICE, SEVENTY-EIGHT MILES (125KM) EAST OF PRAGUE

THE TRACK: RIGHT-HANDED, CHASE COURSE OF FOUR AND A QUARTER MILES (6,900M), HURDLES/FLAT COURSE OF A MILE AND THREE FURLONGS (2,220M); RACING FROM MAY TO OCTOBER

PRINCIPAL RACES: VELKÁ PARDUBICKÁ, OCTOBER
OPENED: 1856

The industrial eastern Czech city of Pardubice is home to the manufacturer of Semtex, and to a horse race which has had, at times, its own incendiary reputation.

At the climax of Pardubice's season, the Velká Pardubická is as gruelling a test of the steeplechaser as there is. Staged over a twisting four-and-a-half-mile (7,200m) long cross-country course, made up of approximately seventy-five per cent grass and twenty-five per cent plough – though it used to be more – there are thirty-one obstacles to be negotiated, and hard-luck stories aplenty.

Names, or nicknames, of fences like the 'Snake Ditch' or 'The Moat' probably only add to the aura of the challenge. The most famous fence is the Taxis Ditch. Named in honour of a prince of the Thurn and Taxis house – a defender of its size and difficulty against critics who existed even in the early years – 'the Taxis' is jumped early on, as the fourth. It consists of a thick, five-foot (1.5m) high hedge with a wide, three-foot (1m) deep trench on the landing side; it is widely considered the most fearsome jump in horseracing.

Modifications were made to the dimensions of the obstacles in the early 1990s after public protests, but the race remains the most daunting of challenges. The first staging was won by British-born jockey George Sayers riding Fantome, and now as the Czechia's longest surviving sporting event, it makes a national hero of any winner. No winner is more feted than Josef Váňa senior, the one-

time ski-lift engineer and mountain rescue team member who came to race-riding in his late twenties. In twenty-eight attempts at the Velká Pardubická, which ended at the age of sixty-one, he won on a record eight occasions, four times on the record-breaking Zeleznik.

Few sportspeople can ever have been as tough as Váňa, who was once declared dead after a fall, and who believes there is hardly a bone in his body that has not at some point been broken. A life-size bronze of him stands at the course where he so dominated in the saddle.

After retirement – when injury finally caught up with him – Váňa turned his attention to training, and he has already excelled in his country's famous race, so much so that a second statue may soon have to be commissioned.

Klampenborg

Denmark

LOCATION: TWELVE MILES (19.3KM) NORTH OF COPENHAGEN CITY CENTRE

THE TRACK: RIGHT-HANDED, OVAL, TURF COURSE OF A MILE AND ONE FURLONG (1,800M); MEETINGS USUALLY ON SATURDAYS, APRIL–OCTOBER

PRINCIPAL RACES: SCANDINAVIAN OPEN CHAMPIONSHIP, AUGUST

OPENED: 1910

FAMOUS MOMENTS: LESTER PIGGOTT WINS THE INAUGURAL SCANDINAVIAN OPEN CHAMPIONSHIP IN 1977 ABOARD TRAINER'S SEAT, THEN RETURNS TO BEAT THAT HORSE THE FOLLOWING YEAR ABOARD POLLERTON

Probably Scandinavia's most beautiful racecourse as well as its oldest, Klampenborg is situated in one of Copenhagen's most affluent northern suburbs, just twenty minutes away from the city centre by train. It is surrounded by woodland as it borders the Dyrehaven, or 'deer park', a UNESCO World Heritage site of ancient oak trees and open countryside, where royalty hunted in the seventeenth century. Hansel and Gretel-style cottages peek out from spots around the grassy racecourse and the buildings themselves, many of them red-panelled, add to a rather magical setting.

While by no means one of Denmark's most popular sports – this is its only course – racing has its place in society and racegoers flock there during the summer months if not distracted by a visit to the nearby Bellevue Beach, a popular and stylish coastal spot. The track itself has a couple of neat and modern grandstands following a refurbishment in 2014, with races usually contested between local trainers and challengers from Norway and Sweden.

The Scandinavian Open Championship has become the only Danish Group race recognised by the International Pattern Committee, while the Danish Jockey Club Cup and Danish Pokallob are the only two to have been awarded Listed status in recent times.

While the big race disappeared off the map for nearly two decades after Lester Piggott's appearances in the early years, British trainers returned in the mid-1990s, with Harbour Dues and jockey Pat Eddery memorably leading home a British one-two-three in 1997, before the winner went on to post a highly respectable fourth place in the Melbourne Cup. There have been rather fewer non-Scandinavian visitors in recent years.

Dano-Mast, who won a maiden race at Klampenborg in 1999, went on to not only win many of the prizes that his home track had to offer, but also took the Prix Jean de Chaudenay and Prix Dollar in France, and acted as a fine global ambassador for trainer Flemming Poulsen.

Occasional star names such as Frankel's rider Tom Queally are recruited for the Danish Derby meeting while the country has recently been able to boast its own notable jockey-export in Kevin Stott. Stott, whose British father Ken became a trainer in Copenhagen, has gone on to settle successfully as a rider in Britain.

Auteuil

France

LOCATION: 16TH ARRONDISSEMENT, PARIS, ON THE EDGE OF THE
BOIS DE BOULOGNE
THE TRACK: ELONGATED FIGURE OF EIGHT, LEVEL,
TWO CHASE COURSES OF JUST OVER AND JUST UNDER A MILE AND
THREE FURLONGS (2,239M / 2,166M) AND HURDLES COURSE OF ONE
AND A HALF MILES (2,418M)

PRINCIPAL RACES: GRAND STEEPLECHASE DE PARIS, MAY;
GRANDE COURSE DE HAIES, JUNE
OPENED: 1873

Auteuil is the principal track for the thriving jump racing industry in France. Many French-bred horses, whose stamina and jumping ability – nurtured from a young age – make them popular with buyers on the National Hunt circuits of Britain and Ireland, have cut their teeth at Auteuil.

Races take place over large bush hurdles or a variety of steeplechase obstacles that include hedges, the formidable, almost six-foot (1.75m) bullfinch, and a water jump with a twenty-foot (6m) span. The going is often soft or heavy.

The Fellow completed a rare double by winning the 1991 staging of the 'Grand Steeple' and, in 1994, the Cheltenham Gold Cup, Britain's top steeplechase. In 1962 the British-trained star Mandarin won the same two races, despite his jockey Fred Winter having virtually no control at Auteuil when the bit in the horse's mouth broke early on. On a less happy note, in 1986, Dawn Run, the legendary Irish race-mare, died in a fall in the Grand Course de Haies.

Amidst Auteuil's elegant stands and well-manicured grounds stands a bronze of Al Capone – the horse – who was successful in November's Prix La Haye Jousselin seven times from 1993 to 1999.

Chantilly

France

LOCATION: IN OISE DEPARTMENT, TWENTY-FOUR MILES (38.6KM)
NORTH OF PARIS

THE TRACK: RIGHT-HANDED, FIVE TRACKS IN ALL, WITH CHUTES;
TURF AND POLYTRACK; MAIN COURSE ONE AND A HALF MILES (2,400M)
WITH THREE-FURLONG (600M) HOME STRAIGHT; RACING JANUARY–JULY,
SEPTEMBER–DECEMBER

PRINCIPAL RACES: PRIX DU JOCKEY CLUB, PRIX DE DIANE, BOTH JUNE
OPENED: 1834

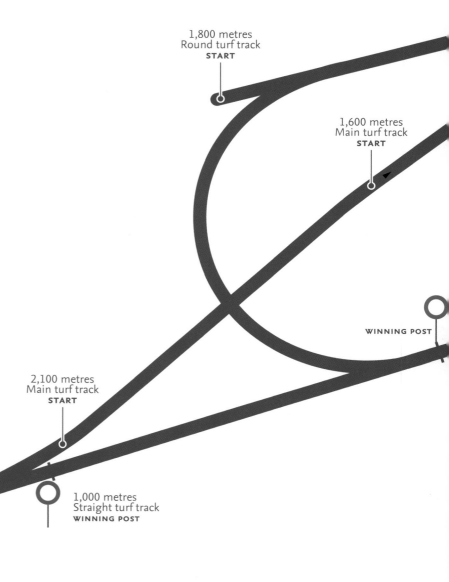

1,800 metres
Round turf track
START

1,600 metres
Main turf track
START

WINNING POST

2,100 metres
Main turf track
START

2,400 metres
Main turf track
START

1,000 metres
Straight turf track
WINNING POST

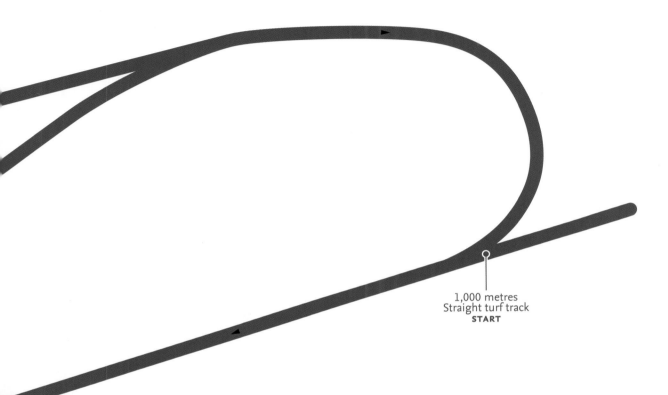

1,000 metres
Straight turf track
START

Racecourse officials around the globe have a wide variety of potential problems to grapple with, but dealing with the antics of wild boar is, to say the least, unusual – though not at Chantilly.

The animals inhabit areas of the hundreds of acres of ancient woodland that are a feature of the Chantilly area, and which initially attracted aristocrats to the region for hunting. Ground staff had to carry out urgent repairs to the racing surface because of damage caused by boars only days before the important Arc Trials fixture in September 2017. Three weeks later the course staged France's premier race, the Prix de l'Arc de Triomphe, for the second year running while its traditional home at ParisLongchamp was renovated and rebranded.

Reminders of Chantilly's noble past are everywhere: the dreamily beautiful chateau, with lake, largely destroyed in the French Revolution but rebuilt a century later; while 'great' does not begin to describe the Grandes Écuries, the royal stables. Commissioned in 1719 by Louis Henri, Duc de Bourbon, who supposedly believed he would be reincarnated as a horse, there is room for 240 equines and double the number of hounds. The stunning building by the architect Jean Aubert dominates the far side of the racecourse; these days, it houses works of art in the Living Museum of the Horse, while the chateau itself is home to the Musée Condé.

The buildings featured in the 1980s James Bond movie *A View To A Kill* as home to the horse-loving villain Max Zorin, who takes part in a frenetic steeplechase against 007, played by Roger Moore. In contrast, in real life at Chantilly, the racing is all staged on the Flat, and the atmosphere is commendably serene.

It all started in the early-to-mid-eighteenth century when races across the lawn of the chateau were formalised with an official fixture in May 1834. In 1847, two permanent stands were erected; they were replaced in the 1880s, after which the weighing room and other facilities were developed.

The course's two best-known races, the Prix du Jockey Club and the Prix de Diane, were introduced within a decade of the first official fixture. Although their distances have been reduced by just under a quarter-mile (300m) from the traditional Classic distance of a mile and a half (2,400m), the Prix du Jockey Club – named in honour of the eponymous organisation at Newmarket – and the Prix de Diane are considered France's equivalent of the Derby and Oaks.

Two British-born brothers, Henry and Tom Jennings – sons of a Cambridgeshire innkeeper – who had arrived at Chantilly as teenagers, made the biggest early impression on the two feature races. Part of a large number of Britons who settled as trainers, jockeys and stable staff in the area, the Jenningses combined to win the first staging of the Prix de Diane with Nativa, trained by Henry and ridden by Tom. In all, Henry – whose daughter Henrietta married William Head, father of Alec and grandfather of Criquette and Freddy, thereby spawning a whole dynasty of French trainer-breeders – saddled the winning filly a total of nine times; Tom was responsible for the successful horse in the Prix du Jockey Club on ten occasions.

Racing at Chantilly was interrupted by war in the 1870s and again between 1915 and 1918, but the biggest impact was when the Nazis invaded France in 1940 and Chantilly was used as an airbase. Many members of the burgeoning ex-pat community either fled or were interned, and leading horses, including the 1939 Prix du Jockey Club winner Pharis, were forcibly removed to Germany to be mated with mares at the National Stud.

In the 1990s, different hard times prevailed, and closure was threatened, but a consortium including racehorse owner and breeder the Aga Khan and other local figures and organisations ensured its future.

A major refurbishment was carried out in the first decade of the new century, and the development of Chantilly received an official seal of approval when the Prix de l'Arc de Triomphe was moved to the track in 2016 and 2017. Both stagings were won by fillies, with Found (2016) leading home a remarkable 1-2-3 in the race for trainer Aidan O'Brien, the Coolmore racing and thoroughbred breeding operation and its prolific stallion Galileo.

The two-year move from Longchamp was considered a fine success, and Chantilly can be said to be thriving as both a racecourse and training centre. More racing than ever is taking place at Chantilly after the opening of an artificial track in 2012; around 3,000 horses are in training in the area; and the visitors keep on coming for the races and the sights.

Deauville-La Touques
France

LOCATION: NORMANDY COAST, 125 MILES (201.2KM) NORTHWEST OF PARIS

THE TRACK: RIGHT-HANDED, OVAL, MAINLY LEVEL; TURF TRACK OF A MILE AND THREE FURLONGS (2,200M) WITH CHUTE; SYNTHETIC TRACK OF JUST OVER ONE AND A QUARTER MILES (2,100M)

PRINCIPAL RACES: PRIX MORNY, PRIX JACQUES LE MAROIS, BOTH IN AUGUST

OPENED: 1864

The Group One Prix Morny is Deauville's most significant race for two-year-olds, and it is named after the most significant figure in the creation of the track on France's north coast. The Duc de Morny, an illegitimate half-brother of Emperor Napoleon III, was a prominent player in French politics and business in the mid-nineteenth century, as well as being a lover of the arts and of horseracing.

The duc and his associates purchased an area of marshy land adjacent to La Touques river in Normandy with a plan to create a resort that was more elite than nearby Trouville, where overcrowding had become an increasing problem during the summer months. With the beautiful architecture that he demanded, sandy beaches and a relaxed, exclusive atmosphere – all of which have survived into the twenty-first century – plus the extension of the railway system to the area, it did not take long for the resort to gain popularity amongst the crème de la crème of Paris's social set.

The duc, who also helped to establish Paris's principal racing venue at Longchamp, added the racecourse to the town so fast that, so local legend has it, it was completed before the town's church was holding services. He died soon afterwards but is remembered to this day with the three-quarter-mile (1,200m) Prix Morny, one of European racing's most important two-year-old races, staged as one of the highlights of the high-summer season.

A string of outstanding juveniles have won the race, including Corrida, Blushing Groom, Arazi, Zafonic and the American pair No Nay Never and Lady Aurelia.

Other Group One highlights of Deauville in August are the Prix Jacques Le Marois, the Prix Jean Romanet, the Prix Maurice de Gheest and the Prix Rothschild, all named, like the Prix Morny, after leading figures in the success of the track.

The Jacques Le Marois, staged over the straight one-mile (1,600m), and a 'win and you're in' race for the Breeders' Cup Mile in North America in the autumn, is amongst the most significant races of its type in Europe. Winners have included Miesque and Spinning World – both of whom took the prize twice – Dubai Millennium and Goldikova.

Miesque, trained by Francois Boutin for Stavros Niarchos, the multi-millionaire shipping magnate, was one of racing's best and most adored fillies. Ridden by champion jockey Freddy Head, scion of the successful French Flat racing dynasty, she won the 1000 Guineas in both Britain and France in 1987, although it was her exploits on the other side of the Atlantic that raised her reputation to its highest.

In 1987 and 1988 – the same years that she took the Jacques Le Marois – Miesque saw off a formidable group of opponents to win the Breeders' Cup Mile, first at the now-defunct Hollywood Park in California and then at Churchill Downs in Kentucky.

Head, whose family's historic stud farm – the Haras du Quesnay – is only a few miles outside Deauville, has the distinction of also training winners of the Jacques Le Marois from his base in the Chantilly racing centre. They include Goldikova, also a four-time winner of the Prix Rothschild, and even more successful than

Miesque at the Breeders' Cup with three wins in the Mile race. During the 2008–2010 seasons, Goldikova lined up in three stagings of the mile-race – twice at Santa Anita in California and once at Churchill Downs – and completed an unprecedented hat-trick of wins.

The introduction of a synthetic track at Deauville in 2003 has extended the fixture list into the winter, but the long-held meetings in July and August are the principal attractions, when a day's racing may be celebrated in one of the seaside bars or restaurants followed by a walk along the beach.

Close by Deauville-La Touques is the racetrack at Clairefontaine – officially Deauville-Clairefontaine – created in 1928, and specialising in steeplechasing and hurdling. Other equestrian activities popular in the area include trotting and polo. There are also numerous stud farms taking advantage of the fertile conditions of Normandy to produce high-quality young horses, many of which are sold at Deauville's Arqana auction house during the prestigious sales of yearlings that take place in August and October.

It is pretty much exactly what the duc and his partners had in mind.

ParisLongchamp
France

LOCATION: IN THE BOIS DE BOULOGNE, ABOUT SIX AND A HALF MILES (10.5KM) FROM THE CENTRE OF PARIS

THE TRACK: RIGHT-HANDED, OVAL-SHAPED, TURF; GRANDE PISTE COURSE OF A MILE AND THREE-QUARTERS (2,750M), MOYENNE PISTE COURSE OF A MILE AND A HALF (2,500M), PETITE PISTE COURSE OF A MILE AND A THIRD (2,150M), NOUVEAU PISTE COURSE OF SEVEN FURLONGS (1,400M), AND LIGNE DROITE COURSE OF FIVE FURLONGS (1,000M); 547-YARD (500M) HOME STRAIGHT; RACING FROM APRIL TO JULY AND DURING SEPTEMBER AND OCTOBER

PRINCIPAL RACES: PRIX DE L'ARC DE TRIOMPHE, OCTOBER; GRAND PRIX DE PARIS, JULY; POULE D'ESSAI DES POULICHES/POULAINS, MAY

OPENED: 1857

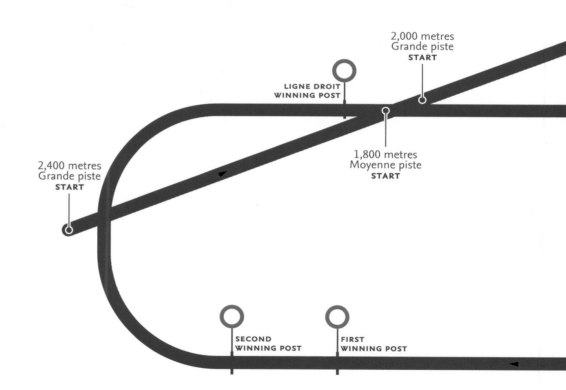

2,000 metres
Grande piste
START

LIGNE DROIT
WINNING POST

2,400 metres
Grande piste
START

1,800 metres
Moyenne piste
START

SECOND
WINNING POST

FIRST
WINNING POST

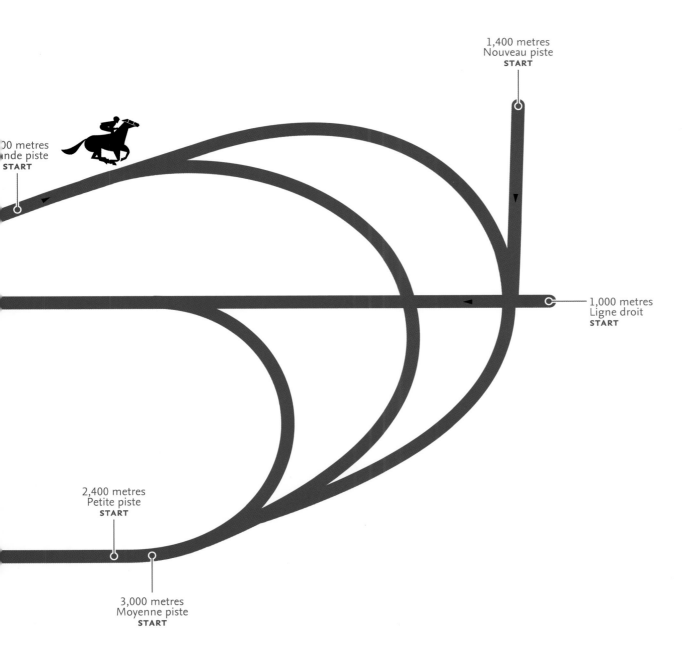

1,400 metres
Nouveau piste
START

00 metres
nde piste
START

1,000 metres
Ligne droit
START

2,400 metres
Petite piste
START

3,000 metres
Moyenne piste
START

With two finishing posts in use – plus a third if you include the separate sprint course – and a 'false' straight before the runners hit the final finishing run, the racecourse at ParisLongchamp has been known to cause mix-ups for jockeys. There is no such confusion, however, when it comes to the quality of France's premier Flat-racing venue.

Set in 141 acres in the picturesque Bois de Boulogne, on the western side of Paris and with the Eiffel Tower rising proudly in the distance, the course displays much of the style for which its home country is so renowned. Such characteristics famously attracted Impressionist artists including Degas and Manet, but while most of the grand old stand which they saw was replaced in the 1960s, a small section is protected by law and remains. It stands as a monument to the past, next to the extensive modern facilities opened in 2018.

The multi-million-euro building project led to the course's temporary closure in late 2015, and the switching of many of its major races, notably the Group One Prix de l'Arc de Triomphe – 'the Arc' – to Chantilly for two years. At the centre of the redevelopment is a four-storey stand, designed by the world-renowned architect Dominique Perrault, with magnificent 360-degree views across the city, and a capacity of 10,000.

To coincide with the launch of the 'new Longchamp' a change of name, to ParisLongchamp, was made. Unchanged, however, is the high-tree-lined paddock, as beautiful as it is iconic, and the distinctive windmill, built on the site of a medieval original on the edge of the course. There are no alterations either to the track or, more accurately, to the five tracks which make up Longchamp and which allow for forty-six possible race starts.

On 'Arc weekend', 50,000-plus attend, but many are British and Irish visitors, and one of the big talking points about racing in France is why it is unable to more regularly attract the home-grown crowds it deserves.

First staged at Longchamp in 1920, the Arc has become the premier horse race in Europe and, it could be reasonably argued, the world. For three-year-olds and older, it takes place over one and a half miles (2,400m) on an early October weekend that features a total of nine Group One races, regularly crowning champions.

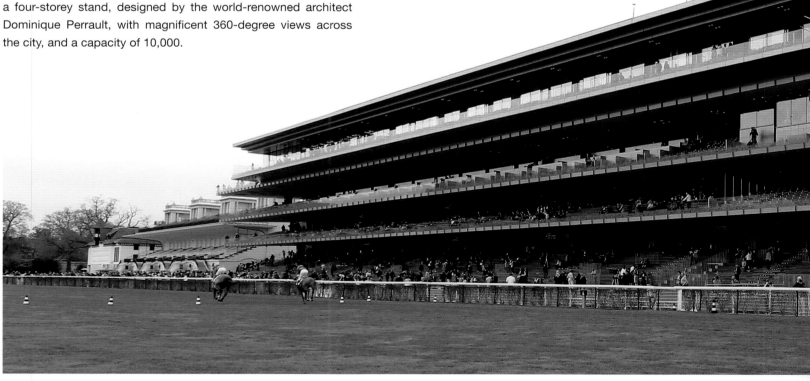

Some of Flat racing's biggest names have recorded memorable wins: Ribot in 1955 and 1956; the peerless Sea-Bird, against a high-quality field in 1965; in 1971, the Epsom Derby winner Mill Reef; Dancing Brave stormed home in 1986; and the brilliant filly Treve in 2013 and 2014.

Pre-dating the Arc by more than half a century is Longchamp's Grand Prix de Paris, nowadays staged on Bastille Day, 14th July, also over one and a half miles (2,400m). The Grand Prix was the course's original feature event, and in its third year was famously won by Gladiateur, French-owned and bred, but trained in Britain.

The horse was nicknamed 'The Avenger of Waterloo' as he added the Grand Prix de Paris to victories in the 2000 Guineas at Newmarket and the Epsom Derby. Success in that year's St Leger – so the Triple Crown – and in the 1866 Gold Cup at Royal Ascot followed, to ensure the horse a special place in French

racing history, plus a statue and a race – the Prix Gladiateur, in September.

Because of war, the Grand Prix was cancelled in 1871, and again in 1915–16; in 1939 and 1940, the Arc was called off. Otherwise, however, racing continued during the Second World War, even though the Germans used the track for placing anti-aircraft guns.

In 1943, a daytime air raid, targeting the nearby Renault factory, saw Longchamp racegoers running for cover as bombs fell while

a racing fixture took place below. Seven people died, but – it is hard to know whether to be impressed at the stoicism or appalled – after just a brief interlude the meeting continued with the runners in the Prix des Sablons navigating around bomb craters. The race, now the Prix Ganay and a significant Group One prize in the early season, was moved to nearby Maisons-Laffitte for the rest of the War. Other races moved across Paris to Le Tremblay but returned home in 1945 where they all stayed until the temporary closure which signalled the ushering in of the 'new Longchamp' of 2018.

Hoppegarten

Germany

LOCATION: TWELVE MILES (19.3KM) EAST OF BERLIN

THE TRACK: RIGHT-HANDED, OVAL, TURF, ONE AND A HALF MILES (2,350M) ROUND WITH CHUTE, QUARTER-MILE-PLUS (550M) HOME STRAIGHT; RACING APRIL—OCTOBER

PRINCIPAL RACES: GROSSER PREIS VON BERLIN, AUGUST

OPENED: 1868

Few racecourses can have fallen from grace quite as dramatically as Hoppegarten, but reclaiming former glories is a dream again.

Set on a former hop farm surrounded by forest to the east of Berlin, heavy investment meant that the new track and training centre at Hoppegarten became the most important place in German racing after it opened in 1868. Most of the country's major prizes were staged there, and between the First and Second World Wars the racing fixtures were the height of fashion, with visitors catered for in well-appointed stands. Around 1,000 horses were prepared on the neighbouring training grounds.

In the 1930s the Nazis supported Hoppegarten, and Hitler guaranteed funding. Racing continued until 1944, when the site became a munitions factory and a target for bombing raids. At the end of the war, redrawn boundaries meant that the course was now in East Germany, and while racing in West Germany continued to go about its business, behind the Iron Curtain it struggled. Various competitions took place between Soviet Bloc countries, moving around from venue to venue, but it was low-grade stuff.

Everything changed with the fall of the Berlin Wall in 1989. For years afterwards, people spoke fondly of the German-German Race Day, held in March 1990 as part of the celebrations, when thousands descended on Hoppegarten to enjoy the racing.

Disputes over ownership led to privatisation in 2008 when the racecourse was taken over by financier Gerhard Schöningh, who has ambitions to return it to a place at the top. Under Schöningh management, Hoppegarten's reputation as a racecourse has grown, along with all-important betting turnover and visitor numbers; a feel-good factor is back for the first time in years.

The historic Grosser Preis von Berlin – staged by the Nazis as the Grand Prix Reichshauptstadt (Imperial State) – came back to its original home in 2011, having journeyed over the years to Düsseldorf and Hamburg. That first year, the race was won by brilliant German filly Danedream. Twelve months later trainer Roland Dzubasz became the first based at Hoppegarten to be German champion since reunification. And a tie-up with the New York Racing Association promises more international runners. Hoppegarten is now even listed as a German Landmark of National Importance; the dream is on.

Baden-Baden

Germany

LOCATION: IFFEZHEIM, SEVEN MILES (11.3KM) FROM BADEN-BADEN, CLOSE TO THE BORDER WITH FRANCE

THE TRACK: LEFT-HANDED, OVAL, FLAT, ONE AND A QUARTER MILES (2,000M) ROUND AND SEPARATE SPRINT COURSE, 547-YARD (500M) HOME STRAIGHT

PRINCIPAL RACES: GROSSER PREIS VON BADEN, SEPTEMBER

OPENED: 1858

The supposed healing qualities of the baths at Baden-Baden have drawn visitors to the resort for centuries, but the problem for the rich nineteenth-century tourists was that there were only so many immersions in hot water, theatre visits and scenic walks they could take. And so, in the 1850s the local casino owner, Frenchman Edouard Bénazet, decided to branch out into horseracing and found a site at the village of Iffezheim, a few miles to the north.

The French racing authorities oversaw its administration until France lost the six-month Franco-Prussian War of 1870–71, after which the Internationaler Club took over. Until the creation of the Baden Racing Company in 2010, the Internationaler Club dedicated itself to raising the profile of horseracing at Iffezheim. It established the three distinct events that are staged every year: the Spring Festival at the end of May; the Grosse Woche ('big week') in late August/early September; and the Sales and Racing Festival, alongside the yearling sales, in October.

Grosse Woche features the Group One Grosser Preis von Baden, German racing's showpiece over one and a half miles (2,400m) for three-year-olds and older. It has been won by a long and distinguished list of European star-names, though perhaps two in particular stand out. With an extraordinary career of fifty-four races contested and fifty-four races won, including a hat-trick at

Baden-Baden between 1877 and 1879, Kincsem is the undisputed star of Hungarian racing history. The equivalent in Germany is Danedream, trained by Peter Schiergen and winner of the Baden-Baden highlight in 2011 and 2012.

A bargain-basement buy, Danedream rose up to become European Champion Three-Year-Old Filly in 2011, winning the Prix de l'Arc de Triomphe at Longchamp in Paris the same year, and the King George VI and Queen Elizabeth Stakes at Ascot the following summer. In 2012, in front of a large and noisy crowd at Iffezheim, she was forced to work hard to win the Grosser Preis von Baden for a second time, a race that turned out to be her swansong. An outbreak of disease at the Cologne racing centre saw Danedream barred from taking part in the defence of her Prix de l'Arc de Triomphe title, and she was retired to stud.

Despite the success of the feature race, and the good reputation of the thoroughbred breeding industry in Germany, betting turnover across the country has fallen dramatically: gamblers prefer football. Iffezheim has had to weather its own economic storms but survive it has since a restructuring carried out under the management of Baden Racing. And they didn't even need a dip in the baths.

Markopoulo

Greece

LOCATION: TWENTY MILES (32.3KM) SOUTHEAST OF CENTRAL ATHENS

THE TRACK: RIGHT-HANDED, OVAL, SAND TRACK OF ABOUT A MILE AND TWO FURLONGS (1,950M); MEETINGS THREE TIMES A WEEK THROUGHOUT THE YEAR, EXCEPT AUGUST

PRINCIPAL RACES: GREEK DERBY, JULY

OPENED: 2004

FAMOUS MOMENTS: IALYSOS, UNBEATEN IN SEVEN STARTS BETWEEN 2007 AND 2009, BEING DUBBED THE 'GREEK FREAK' BY HIS NEXT TRAINER LUCA CUMANI WHEN THE COLT WON IN BRITAIN

Horseracing was probably founded by the Ancient Greeks, and Greece is steeped in equine tradition. The previous main racecourse, by the seafront near the port of Piraeus, had some good times during its seventy-eight years of activity, even if facilities had become dilapidated by the end. With the 2004 Athens Olympics came the development of extensive facilities required for the equestrian events. As part of a £200 million project, a brand-new racecourse was included at the Markopoulo site, close to the Aegean Sea.

At least there was some forward thinking; many purpose-built centres for the likes of canoeing, softball and beach volleyball have been pictured in news outlets lying abandoned and derelict since the games finished. Not only was the financial crash a factor, they were also superfluous to the Greek sporting public's needs.

Racehorse trainers found themselves with 1,600 state-of-the-art stables from which to operate and a racecourse with a capacity of 8,000. However, in the years following the Olympics, state-owned Markopoulo was blighted by mis-management and gambling legislation issues, and by the fact that the venue was far more difficult to access than the old course at the Delta of Faliro. These factors have all led to a drop in spectator numbers. What could

be a world-class track, with a good surface, neat grandstand and pretty views into the hills, does not have the public interest it deserves and there are often just a handful of people rattling around in it.

It is subsidised by only a few, and one of the country's most famous racehorse-owning sons was better known for supporting trainers elsewhere. Shipping tycoon Stavros Niarchos, who won races around the world with horses like the outstanding Miesque, tended to concentrate on racing in France, Britain and America. His family has followed suit.

One great supporter was George Cambanis, who in 1953 established Figaia Stud, which has produced many fine horses, including the sprinter Ialysos. Cambanis' daughter Marina Marinopoulos and her husband Leonidas have maintained the tradition, keeping an extensive string in France and Britain, as well as in Athens. Many of their horses have won the Greek Derby, which has been going for more than seventy years and still draws a large, fashionable crowd each July. The 2017 race saw a first success by a female trainer, as Irene Keratsa's Irish-bred Youtalkingtome took the top honours.

Kincsem Park

Hungary

LOCATION: FOUR AND A HALF MILES (7.4KM) EAST OF CENTRAL BUDAPEST

THE TRACK: RIGHT-HANDED, LEVEL OVAL OF A MILE AND A QUARTER (2,000M) ON GRASS, WITH A SIX-AND-A-HALF-FURLONG (1,300M) SPRINT TRACK AND SAND TRACK ON THE INSIDE; MEETINGS HELD APRIL—OCTOBER PLUS TROTTING AND GREYHOUND RACES

PRINCIPAL RACES: MAGYAR DERBY, JULY

OPENED: 1925

FAMOUS MOMENTS: THE FAREWELL PERFORMANCE IN 2010 OF OVERDOSE, HUNGARY'S GREATEST HORSE OF MODERN TIMES

Hungary's only racecourse is named after its greatest ever horse. Kincsem became a national icon, but was clearly an extraordinary performer, not least for the amount of travelling she did to race. Unbeaten in fifty-five starts during a gruelling four-year campaign from 1876, she won in Eastern Europe, of course, but was also taken to Britain's Goodwood Cup and to the Grand Prix de Deauville in France. There was national mourning when Kincsem died of a colic attack on her thirteenth birthday; she has her own museum just west of Budapest. Both Kincsem and Imperial, another mighty horse of the nineteenth century, have statues at the course.

The course is a green lung of the capital, easily accessible by the metro system. The track itself is fairly featureless as a flat, grass oval, but an extensive revamp in 2005 brought with it a modern grandstand which stands in front of the older entrance building. Organisers have been inventive enough to add various initiatives to race-days to broaden their appeal. This has included trotting races, hurdles and even greyhound races, often all held at the same fixture. All ends of the spectrum are catered for, from a grand panoramic restaurant to food trucks for the hipsters and picnickers.

Hard times in Hungarian racing were to some large extent erased by Overdose. Overdose was bought for just 2,000 guineas at Tattersalls Sales in Newmarket in 2006 by owner Zoltan Mikoczy, and became a national star. He was an astonishing sprinter, assembling an unbeaten run of fourteen, not only at home but later from appearances in Austria, Slovakia, Germany and Italy.

Overdose 'won' the Group One Prix de l'Abbaye on Prix de l'Arc de Triomphe day at Longchamp of 2008 in a very fast time with one of his characteristically dominant performances, only for the race to be declared void because of a chaotic start. He did not take part in the re-run later in the day. In Hungary, the 'Wunderpferd' or 'Miracle Horse', who carried the red, white and green silks of the country's flag, retained his reputation, and thousands turned out to see his return at Kincsem Park in 2009. Despite injury problems, Overdose still managed to finish fourth in a race at Royal Ascot; after retirement he went to stud in Germany but died soon after of colic.

Curragh
Ireland

LOCATION: IN COUNTY KILDARE, ABOUT THIRTY-THREE MILES (53KM) WEST-SOUTHWEST OF DUBLIN

THE TRACK: RIGHT-HANDED, HORSESHOE-SHAPED, SWEEPING BENDS, MILD UNDULATIONS; TWO MILES (3,219M), WITH EXTENSION FOR RACES FROM FIVE FURLONGS (1,000M) TO ONE MILE (1,600M); HOME STRAIGHT OF THREE FURLONGS (600M); RACING FROM MARCH TO OCTOBER

PRINCIPAL RACES: HOME TO ALL OF THE IRISH CLASSICS

OPENED: THE FIRST OFFICIALLY RECORDED RACE WAS IN 1727

The Curragh plain is a vast area of ancient natural grassland which contains an army camp as well as Ireland's premier racecourse and its biggest training centre, with around twenty per cent of the country's racehorses being prepared there.

It used to be said that the Curragh's 5,000 acres could comfortably accommodate the army, the various racing interests and the local hunts without anyone getting in each other's way. In 1943, equine and military interests came together when entrance to the Irish Derby was granted to bored German and British prisoners of war – automatically interned at the camp after landing in neutral Ireland, whatever the circumstances – as long as they gave written assurances of their return to the camp.

Racing has taken place in the large open spaces of the Curragh since who knows when: the area was popular for gatherings, and probably chariot racing, perhaps as far back as AD 200. Horseracing as a formal entity can be traced to 1727. The Irish Derby was first staged in 1866 over a mile and three-quarters (2,800m), reduced to the traditional mile-and-a-half (2,400m) Derby distance in 1872; the Oaks followed in 1895 and the St Leger in 1915, but Ireland did not get its full complement of Classics until the two Guineas races were started up in the 1920s.

Today, most of the country's major Flat races take place at the Curragh during the eight-month season, though a major development at the track limited fixtures in 2017 and 2018.

In 1907, the Irish-trained Orby was the first horse to win both the Epsom Derby and the Irish Derby, usually staged a month apart in June. It took more than fifty years for Santa Claus to repeat the feat in 1964; the great trainer Vincent O'Brien, who won the Irish Derby on six occasions, completed the Epsom-Curragh double with Nijinsky (1970) and The Minstrel (1977). Nijinsky, along with Ireland's pioneering 1993 Melbourne Cup hero Vintage Crop, is honoured with a statue at the track.

During the 1960s and 1970s, the Derby's reputation grew rapidly, and with the support of Coolmore, the Irish-based – but globally successful – racing and thoroughbred breeding superpower led by John Magnier, it has risen further. The record-breaking list of Irish Derby wins by Coolmore's principal trainer Aidan O'Brien – no relation to Vincent – includes Galileo (2001) and Camelot (2012), both of whom also won at Epsom. Horses owned by the Coolmore operation and trained by O'Brien have won all of the Irish Classics at the Curragh – including all in the same season in 2008 – as well as dominating all other major races. And there is no sign of that domination ending.

Laytown

Ireland

LOCATION: ON THE COAST, TWENTY-SEVEN MILES (43.5KM) NORTH OF DUBLIN

THE TRACK: COURSE OF UP TO SEVEN FURLONGS (1,400M) ON THE BEACH; ONE FIXTURE IN SEPTEMBER

OPENED: 1868

Horseracing around the world prides itself on its variety of settings. In cities, up mountains, in forests, in deserts, you name it; however, only one, at least in a major jurisdiction, is located on a beach like Laytown, up the coast from the Irish capital Dublin. Unassuming and picturesque for the rest of the year, the miles of sands at Laytown are transformed for one day in September.

Once the tide starts to go out, those in charge race to lay out their track; meanwhile, an array of tents and vehicles are spread across the grassy raised dunes and beyond – famously the only permanent building is one containing some loos. Reminding us that this is an official fixture, whatever the surroundings are, is a temporary weighing room for jockeys and administrators, a sponsors' tent and a paddock. All around are the catering and betting outlets needed for a crowd, usually these days around 5,000.

Racing started on the beach at Laytown in the 1860s to coincide with a prestigious rowing regatta: one could take place when the tide was in, the other when it was out. The day, at one point managed by a priest in defiance of his bishop, became one of the most popular social occasions across the area. Records indicate that the local MP Charles Stewart Parnell, the great Irish Home

Rule campaigner, was an early example of the tradition of Irish politicians mixing business with their horseracing pleasure – many a Taoiseach has been seen standing in a queue for the bookies – by acting as a steward.

All the 'fun of the fair' was attracted to Laytown, the last remaining of a number of places in Ireland that had staged horse races on the beach, and visitors, traders and bookmakers mingled happily alongside the horses and jockeys. Up, that is, until 1994 when an accident took place at Laytown, putting this most distinctive of racing fixtures in jeopardy. With races as long as two miles (3,200m), the runners had always had to negotiate a very tight bend on the U-shaped course, but that year a pile-up took place which led to horse fatalities, injuries to jockeys and fears for the safety of spectators.

Although the Irish authorities were happy to permit races to continue at Laytown, they did insist on changes, notably a straight course only was to be used, and the public was to be moved back out of harm's way. So now a six-race card containing two over six furlongs (1,200m) and four over seven (1,400) makes up the programme, but what a course and what a setting.

Leopardstown
Ireland

LOCATION: SIX MILES (9.7KM) SOUTH OF CENTRAL DUBLIN

THE TRACK: LEFT-HANDED, ALMOST RECTANGULAR, FLAT AND NATIONAL HUNT ON TURF, CIRCUIT OF JUST UNDER A MILE AND THREE-QUARTERS (2,800M) WITH THREE-FURLONG (600M) HOME STRAIGHT; FLAT APRIL–OCTOBER, NATIONAL HUNT DECEMBER–MARCH

PRINCIPAL RACES: IRISH CHAMPION STAKES, SEPTEMBER; DUBLIN RACING FESTIVAL, FEBRUARY

OPENED: 1888

FAMOUS MOMENTS: THE GREAT INTERNATIONAL JOCKEY MICK KINANE RIDES HIS FIRST-EVER WINNER, MUSCARI, AT LEOPARDSTOWN, MARCH 1975; LOCATION FOR IRELAND'S FIRST AIR SHOW (1910)

Set in 200 acres of the affluent south Dublin suburb of Foxrock, Leopardstown Racecourse's name has no zoological derivation but originates from its location being on land that was once part of a leper colony. All of which presumably means that it has previously been a far from popular area: how things have changed. Dublin's urban sprawl gets ever closer, as does the city's road network, creating a feeling of being somewhat hemmed in, but it does ensure the track is accessible to more and more people.

Leopardstown, the principal 'dual purpose' – both Flat and National Hunt – course in Ireland, was modelled on Sandown Park in the UK, though the runners actually compete the other way around (left-handed). It is a terrific 'viewing' course, where racegoers can see pretty much every inch of the action from most vantage points, and views of the Irish Sea on one side and the Wicklow Mountains on the other only serve to enhance the spectacle.

The first fixture took place in the summer of 1888 and was so unexpectedly popular that there was all sorts of talk of racegoers not being able to get within striking distance of the course to witness that opening afternoon.

Although the perception might well be that Flat racing at the Curragh and jumping at Punchestown provide Ireland's premier prizes, Leopardstown, the only course in Dublin since Phoenix Park closed in 1990, more than holds its own. The one-and-a-quarter-mile (2,000m) Irish Champion Stakes – originally staged at Leopardstown in the 1970s, but then relocated to 'the Park' from 1984 to 1990 – is regularly one of the most significant Group One-level races of the year. Staged on the first day of September's Irish Champions Weekend – shared with the Curragh – winners have included some of European Flat racing's greatest names, and it has been the stage for some memorable encounters, notably in 2001 when Fantastic Light beat arch-rival Galileo after a breathless duel.

Significant Classic-race dress rehearsals take place in the spring, with May's Derby Trial providing more than its fair share of clues for the main events at Epsom and the Curragh later in the season. Leopardstown's four-day Christmas Festival has long been a feature on the National Hunt calendar, while the widely applauded innovation of the Dublin Racing Festival weekend in February 2018 looks sure to become a significant destination on the trail to the Cheltenham Festival five weeks later.

A magnificent bronze of five-time Irish Champion Hurdler Hurricane Fly (2011–2015) now greets visitors on arrival.

Weekend racing on Sundays is normal practice these days, but in July 1985 it was Leopardstown that staged the first fixture on the Sabbath in Britain or Ireland.

Punchestown

Ireland

LOCATION: TWENTY-FIVE MILES (40.2KM) WEST OF DUBLIN, OUTSIDE NAAS, COUNTY KILDARE

THE TRACK: RIGHT-HANDED, ALMOST SQUARE, CHASE COURSE OF TWO MILES (3,200M) WITH HURDLES TRACK ON INSIDE, SEPARATE CROSS-COUNTRY COURSE; RACING FROM OCTOBER TO JUNE

PRINCIPAL RACES: CHAMPION CHASE, GOLD CUP, CHAMPION HURDLE AT THE IRISH NATIONAL HUNT FESTIVAL, APRIL

OPENED: 1824

The first-ever recognised steeplechase took place in Ireland in 1752 when Edmund Blake and Cornelius O'Callaghan raced their horses across open country for a bet involving a cask of wine. They started at the church in the village of Buttevant, and the winner was the first to clear the banks, ditches, hedges and walls between there and the church four miles (6.4km) away in Doneraile, hence (church) steeplechasing, and indeed point-to-pointing. That heritage continues to be celebrated at Punchestown with races staged on a cross-country course – the only one of its kind in Ireland – in which the runners compete over similar types of jumps.

The La Touche Cup, named after a member of the family that gave the land at Punchestown to the Kildare Hunt Club, is one of the highlights of the festival held every spring. Thirty-five mainly banks and walls must be negotiated, including Ruby's Double, a bank which commemorates the grandfather of champion jockey Ruby Walsh.

Risk Of Thunder, trained by the 'King of the Banks' Enda Bolger for the actor Sean Connery, took the prize a remarkable seven times in a row between 1995 and 2002 (the race was called off in 2001). Punchestown's close ties to jump racing's historic grassroots is further illustrated in the Festival's Bishopscourt Cup, in which only runners owned by farmers in the Kildare Hunt Club area may take part.

The Kildare Hunt Club, some of whose members continue to serve on the racecourse management team, started to hold horseracing, some of it at Punchestown, in the 1820s. The start of what is now the Festival settled full-time at Punchestown in April 1850, and was considered a major social as well as sporting occasion. Four years later, it took on a two-day format which continued until 1963, and three days became four in 1999 after redevelopment work; a fifth day was added in 2008.

Although fixtures are staged throughout the season, the Punchestown Festival in the spring is the big week of the year; following hard on the heels of British racing's biggest festival, it is seen now as an 'Irish Cheltenham', at which many leading horses, particularly from Ireland, but also from Britain, will be aimed. Cheltenham may remain as the 'be-all and end-all' for most National Hunt stalwarts, but Punchestown is not many lengths behind.

Fairyhouse

Ireland

LOCATION: SEVENTEEN MILES (27.4KM) NORTH OF DUBLIN, IN COUNTY MEATH

THE TRACK: RIGHT-HANDED, ALMOST SQUARE-SHAPED, GALLOPING TRACK OF A MILE AND THREE-QUARTERS (2,900M), USED FOR NATIONAL HUNT AND FLAT; MEETINGS THROUGHOUT THE YEAR

PRINCIPAL RACES: IRISH GRAND NATIONAL, EASTER; HATTONS GRACE HURDLE, NOVEMBER

OPENED: 1848

FAMOUS MOMENTS: THE BRILLIANT GREY DESERT ORCHID CARRYING TOP-WEIGHT OF 12 STONES TO VICTORY IN THE 1990 IRISH GRAND NATIONAL

Fairyhouse can be a chilly place to be in the depths of winter. However, on Easter Monday, whatever the weather, it will not stop crowds from the capital crossing the county boundary on what has been traditionally known as the 'Dubs' Day Out' to witness the Irish Grand National.

The highlight of a three-day fixture usually comes close to the Grand National meeting at Aintree, and no horse has ever achieved the double in the same year. It is usually just as competitive as the Aintree race, even if it is over a slightly shorter distance and over standard fences. The likes of Rhyme 'n' Reason and Numbersixvalverde have collected both prizes in different seasons in recent times.

The race takes place on land close to the small County Meath town of Ratoath, first used for point-to-points by the Ward Union Hunt. It was not long before the big race established itself in the social calendar. Indeed, in 1916, 25,000 people were there the day news filtered through of the Easter Rising, when republicans seized a number of key locations in Dublin. As the rebels anticipated, the British Army was caught unawares, with many officers and soldiers enjoying an afternoon away at the races. The British seized all vehicles at the track and shut down the railway line to Dublin, leaving spectators stranded; famously, the winning horse, All Sorts, had to be walked the 60 miles (96.6km) back to his stable in County Westmeath.

In 1929, one of the more extraordinary human performances in the Irish Grand National took place when jockey Frank Wise steered his own horse, Alike, to victory riding with a wooden leg and despite having lost three fingers on his right hand, all the result of injuries received in the Great War.

Trainer Tom Dreaper won the race ten times between 1942 and 1966, including seven in succession from 1960. The list included all-time National Hunt greats Fortria (1961), the legendary Arkle (1964), and in 1966 Flyingbolt, a horse Dreaper believed might have been even better than Arkle but for illness.

Fairyhouse has an uphill finish, and a short run from the last fence, often leading to spectacularly close battles to the winning line. There is top-class racing throughout the Easter Festival, as well as a significant two-day card in late autumn where Cheltenham prospects line up in the Hatton's Grace Hurdle and Drinmore Novice Chase. Flat racing is something of an afterthought here, with nothing like the status of National Hunt, the most notable event being the Group Three Brownstown Stakes.

Capannelle

Italy

LOCATION: EIGHT AND A HALF MILES (13.7KM) SOUTHEAST OF CENTRAL ROME

THE TRACK: RIGHT-HANDED, EXTENDED OVAL; TURF COURSES OF A MILE AND FIVE FURLONGS (2,600M) / A MILE AND A HALF (2,400M) A MILE AND THREE FURLONGS (2,200M), ALL-WEATHER COURSE OF ONE AND A QUARTER MILES (2,000M), AND SPRINT COURSE OF THREE-QUARTERS OF A MILE (1,200M); RACING DURING SPRING AND AUTUMN SEASONS

PRINCIPAL RACES: PREMIO LYDIA TESIO, OCTOBER

OPENED: 1881

FAMOUS MOMENTS: RUNAWAY SUCCESS BY NEARCO IN 1938

Racing at Capannelle has taken some hits in recent years with leading prizes downgraded in terms of quality in the European pattern of major races. The Group One Premio Lydia Tesio, run over a mile and a quarter (2,000m), is the sole top-level race staged in the country these days. For fillies and mares aged three and above, the race remembers Lydia Tesio, who, with her husband Federico, was a huge influence on Italian horseracing during the twentieth century.

The Tesios founded Dormello Stud from where they bred, owned and sometimes trained a string of leading horses, including the winners of twenty-two Derby Italianos at Capannelle, notably Nearco in 1938. Though by winning the Prix de l'Arc de Triomphe at Longchamp, twice, the Tesios' horse Ribot is best known, Nearco has had a more enduring influence on the sport. Undefeated in his fourteen races – three at Capannelle – Nearco was sold to be a stallion in the UK where he had widespread success. Amongst hundreds of winning progeny was Nearctic, who himself sired Northern Dancer, the thoroughbred breeding world's most potent stallion.

Racing started at Capannelle in the late nineteenth century and retains a certain charm, with the Alban Hills in the distance.

Merano

Italy

LOCATION: AT THE SOUTHERN END OF THE SPA TOWN OF MERANO, IN THE FAR NORTH OF ITALY

THE TRACK: RIGHT-HANDED, LEVEL, TURF FLAT-RACING TRACK OF A MILE AND A QUARTER (2,000M), WITH VARIOUS JUMPING COURSES WEAVING AROUND THE INFIELD; RACING FROM EASTER TO OCTOBER

PRINCIPAL RACES: GRAN PREMIO DI MERANO, SEPTEMBER

OPENED: 1935

FAMOUS MOMENTS: A TRULY EXTRAORDINARY MOMENT OF MISFORTUNE EXPERIENCED BY IRISH-BORN JOCKEY CHRIS MEEHAN (SEE BELOW)

It is no surprise that Merano is a popular getaway for Germans and Italians with its handy vineyards and great walking (and skiing) in the picturesque South Tyrol. The town was visited frequently by Empress Elisabeth of Austria in the seventeenth century. She preferred the waters, but the town's racecourse is certainly not to be missed, particularly if visiting at the end of September for the premier meeting.

The Gran Premio di Merano is one of the world's most famous steeplechases. Impressive prize money regularly lures chasers from France, Czechia and even Britain and Ireland, from where trainer Willie Mullins and his jockey Ruby Walsh made an unsuccessful attempt in 2015. Unexpectedly, the race was one of the first major victories of Jim Crowley in 2004 before he switched from jump racing to the Flat, eventually becoming British champion Flat jockey.

The Gran Premio has been around since the track was created in 1935. There had been another racecourse when the region was part of the Austro-Hungarian Empire, but by this stage it had been annexed by Italy. The rationalist-style grandstands were designed by the renowned architect Paolo Vietti-Violi, whose work was seen at many other Italian racetracks, and the project was finished within a year.

While there is some Flat racing, it is secondary to the jumps. Runners in the Gran Premio jump over and through huge live hedges, while the cross-country course is even more striking. Runners splash through water, jump walls and The Big Oxer – which lays claim to be racing's biggest obstacle in the world – and almost leave the racecourse perimeter at one stage to bound over huge man-made banks. Three different and confusing-looking obstacle courses are marked out by privet, giving it the look of Hampton Court's maze from a distance.

Tyrolean tradition comes to the fore in August with the Palio del Burgraviato. This features races between local areas, with some including the region's flaxen Haflinger mountain horses.

Merano is a place that jockey Chris Meehan will never forget. Knocked out briefly and kicked in the face in a fall during a race while on a working holiday in Italy, he found worse was to come. The ambulance that arrived to help him came to a halt on his right leg, breaking that as well. Irony of ironies, Meehan's father was an instructor for ambulance drivers, though not in Italy.

Duindigt

Netherlands

LOCATION: EIGHT MILES (12.9KM) NORTHEAST OF THE HAGUE

THE TRACK: LEFT-HANDED, OVAL-SHAPED, TURF, ONE MILE (1,600M);
LARGELY MIXED MEETINGS OF FLAT AND JUMPS; MARCH TO OCTOBER

PRINCIPAL RACES: GROTE PRIJS DER LAGE LANDEN, JUNE; DUTCH DERBY,
AUGUST

OPENED: 1906

FAMOUS MOMENTS: LAUNCH SITE OF GERMAN V2 ROCKETS IN THE
SECOND WORLD WAR

For all the success of the Netherlands in equestrian disciplines at the Olympics, it is certainly not one of European racing's superpowers. With trotting seemingly the preferred choice of Dutch punters, Duindigt is the only Flat racing track of any consequence.

It is a pleasant place almost entirely surrounded by woodland, with runners picking their way through the trees as they are led onto the course. The area has been part of an estate belonging to the Jochems family for several centuries and Walter Jochems, founder of modern Duindigt, owned not only horses but llamas. Descendants of those shipped from Peru at the turn of the century still live nearby today.

Very few Dutch racing figures have broken into the mainstream, but jockey Adrie de Vries rode his first winner at Duindigt, and claimed numerous national titles before outgrowing the scene and becoming German champion in 2014.

The Dutch Derby is the feature event each August and often attracts runners from Germany as its prize money is competitive with other European Listed races. Purses are not always as generous but there has been a recent boost since Duindigt was added to the international Arabian racing programme.

Øvrevoll

Norway

LOCATION: CLOSE TO THE FORESTS IN THE SUBURBS SEVEN MILES (11.3KM) NORTHWEST OF OSLO

THE TRACK: LEFT-HANDED, UNDULATING, OVAL TURF OF A MILE AND A QUARTER (2,000M), HALF-MILE (800M) HOME STRAIGHT, WITH DIRT CIRCUIT INSIDE; MAINLY FLAT RACING, SOME HURDLES, APRIL–NOVEMBER

PRINCIPAL RACES: OSLO CUP, POLAR CUP, BOTH LATE JULY/EARLY AUGUST; MARIT SVEAAS MINNELOP, AUGUST

OPENED: 1932

FAMOUS MOMENTS: SECOND OSLO CUP WIN BY NOBLE DANCER IN 1976, A GREAT OF NORWEGIAN RACING, LATER A TOP AMERICAN TURF HORSE

It does not take long to get to the fjords or the unspoilt pine forests around Oslo from the capital, and Øvrevoll is something of a gateway to Norway's idyllic nature, even if the area around the country's only racecourse has become residential.

The track was opened by King Haakon VII and Queen Maud and very much resembles a British country racecourse, with uphill bends approaching each end of a hairpin and quick transition back downhill at the exits. The facilities could reasonably be described as a little rough and ready.

Many of the meetings are under the lights and on the artificial circuit, with free entry, but there are a few occasions when the whole place comes to life. A meeting on the Norwegian national day of May 17th sees the first racing on the grass, along with parading horses and carriages and a funfair. The Norwegian Derby meeting in high summer is not only one for the purists but an occasion to dress to impress, with a keenly contested hat competition.

The Derby itself has international 'Listed' status and the day also stages two of Norway's three recognised Group races. The Marit Sveaas Minnelop is the country's most valuable prize and draws all of Scandinavia's top horses. They even used to have a popular Norwegian Grand National here, in which big names including the late Terry Biddlecombe rode. The 1999 winner Trinitro, ridden by Robert Bellamy, went on to the following year's Aintree Grand National as a 100-1 shot, only to make it no further than the first fence. Steeplechasing has since died out at Øvrevoll, but they have a few small-field races over hurdles including a Norwegian Champion Hurdle.

A couple of hundred horses are trained in the area, and a sand gallop has been installed for them to use. Here, the formative years of William Buick, who was brought up in Norway the son of a Scottish father, Walter – an eight-times champion jockey in the country – and a Norwegian mother, Maria, took place. Buick junior is now a well-known international rider but is fondly remembered in his homeland and returns regularly.

It is noticeable that quite a few Brazilian riders have settled now in Oslo, while the multiple champion trainer based at Øvrevoll, Niels Petersen, has been a regular with runners in Dubai.

Służewiec

Poland

LOCATION: FIVE MILES (8KM) SOUTH OF WARSAW CITY CENTRE

THE TRACK: LEFT-HANDED, OVAL, ABOUT ONE AND A HALF MILES (2,400M), MAINLY FLAT RACING ON TURF; RACING FROM APRIL TO NOVEMBER, USUALLY ON SATURDAYS AND SUNDAYS

PRINCIPAL RACES: WIELKA WARSZAWSKA, AUTUMN

OPENED: 1939

Służewiec is the principal of Poland's four racecourses, staging the country's main prizes including the historic Wielka Warszawska – the Great Warsaw Race – and the Polish classic races. There is occasional jump racing.

The opening race-day took place amongst much fanfare in June 1939, but proceedings did not last long as the Nazis' invasion of Poland came just three months later. The racecourse survived the horrors of the Second World War without serious damage, as thousands of Hitler's SS troops were stationed at the course.

The Wielka Warszawska, the country's richest and most prestigious prize, was first staged in 1895, but financial problems caused it to be cancelled from 1905 to 1912, and then after one year back, it was called off again because of the outbreak of war. As a result, Poland's equine community relocated to Ukraine. The race settled at Służewiec in the late 1940s, and has thrived ever since, along with the Polish racing industry as a whole.

Moscow
Russia

LOCATION: THREE MILES (5.4KM) NORTHWEST OF RED SQUARE

THE TRACK: LEFT-HANDED, A MILE AND ONE FURLONG (1800M), SAND; RACING HELD MAY TO SEPTEMBER

PRINCIPAL RACES: RUSSIAN FEDERATION PRESIDENT'S CUP, JUNE

OPENED: 1834

Like the country around it, the Central Moscow Hippodrome has lived a topsy-turvy of existence since its creation in the mid-nineteenth century.

Highly successful prior to the October Revolution of 1917, the races attracted large, fashionable crowds – including the doomed Imperial Family – and generated a lucrative income from betting. An impressive grandstand was constructed between 1896 and 1899 with extravagant architecture and decoration, including statues which are to be found at the modern Hippodrome.

After the revolution, the course was closed from 1918 to 1921, and its buildings and grounds used for military training and public meetings until re-opening with around 150 horses. Fire devastated the stand in the late 1940s and it was rebuilt, only for the sport to gradually lose its popularity and the course to close for nine years in the 1990s.

2004 saw the inception of the Russian Federation President's Stakes – often attended by the country's president – staged over one and a half miles (2,400m), on something of a gala equestrian day in June. Fixtures of thoroughbred and Arab horseracing and trotting take place at the Central Moscow Hippodrome, principally at weekends.

There are also around 600 horses in training at the Hippodrome. Many head south for the winter but a hardy group manage to battle the freezing temperatures and snow to get race-fit.

The feature race-days are increasingly popular events in the Moscow social calendar, including the Radio Monte-Carlo day in May where many racegoers dress up for the enthusiastically-contested Best Hat competition.

Moscow stages versions of the five traditional Classics, and these often feature runners who have contested equivalent events at some of the country's other tracks, including Krasnodar, Pyatigorsk, Rostov-on-Don, and Kazan in Tatarstan.

The course is overseen by the country's Ministry of Agriculture and in 2013 Nikolay Isakov took over the Hippodrome's management, following a distinguished career in the military and with the energy giant Gazprom.

San Sebastián

Spain

LOCATION: IN THE SUBURB OF ZUBIETA, FIVE MILES (8KM) WEST OF THE CITY CENTRE

THE TRACK: VERY SHARP, RIGHT-HANDED, ONE-MILE (1,600M) TURF CIRCUIT WITH 656-YARD (600M) STRAIGHT, INSIDE DIRT TRACK FOR TRAINING; JUNE–SEPTEMBER

PRINCIPAL RACES: COPA DE ORO, AUGUST; GRAN PREMIO DE SAN SEBASTIÁN, SEPTEMBER

OPENED: 1916

FAMOUS MOMENTS: THE 550,000-PESETA PRIZE FOR THE 1922 GRAN PREMIO MAKING IT THE MOST VALUABLE RACE IN THE WORLD IN ITS TIME

They call it the Spanish Deauville and it's not hard to see why. Close to the seaside and a vibrant resort, it also has a relaxed and intimate atmosphere that keeps bringing people back. It was constructed by founder King Alfonso XIII in response to the demand for racing, as the sport had been stopped in France during the First World War. Built on an old aerodrome, it offers striking views of green Basque hills from the small but steep green-coloured grandstands. Easy to access through the Pyrenees, it has been the subject of many visits by European racing tourists before they head off to the unspoiled beaches, grand hotels and Michelin-starred restaurants of the city itself.

Certainly Spanish racing has faded since its glory days in the 1920s, with issues with governance and funding. However, it has continued and the generous prize money at San Sebastián has proved attractive to visiting runners. The front-running Australia Day, a competent hurdler in Britain, made appearances in both the Copa de Oro and the Gran Premio in 2012 and 2013, taking the latter once. The grey's trainer Paul Webber booked the right man for the job in Oscar Urbina, who had already become the first Basque jockey to win the Copa de Oro in 1999, as well as landing the Group One Fillies' Mile at Ascot on Soviet Song during his time working at Newmarket.

There is a valuable gold cup that is the winning owner's to keep if they are lucky to land the Copa de Oro, and the level of prize money makes it one of the most lucrative races of its type in Europe.

Around the tree-lined paddock is a roll of honour of past Gran Premio winners. Perhaps most exalted of all is Royal Gait. He took the 1986 Gran Premio as a three-year-old before controversially being disqualified after finishing 'first' in the 1988 Gold Cup at Royal Ascot, having been adjudged to have caused interference. Royal Gait later moved to trainer James Fanshawe in Newmarket and was successful in the 1992 Champion Hurdle in his first jumps season. Equiano, who won the 2008 King's Stand Stakes at Royal Ascot for Spanish trainer Mauricio Delcher Sanchez, also ran there several times as a young horse.

Bro Park
Sweden

LOCATION: TWENTY-FIVE MILES (40.2KM) NORTH OF STOCKHOLM

THE TRACK: LEFT-HANDED, TURF AND GRASS, A MILE AND A QUARTER (2,000M) WITH CAMBERED TURNS; FLAT RACING ONLY, WITH MEETINGS HELD BETWEEN JULY AND DECEMBER

PRINCIPAL RACES: STOCKHOLM CUP, SEPTEMBER

OPENED: 2016

FAMOUS MOMENTS: STAGING THE FIRST LADY JOCKEYS' THOROUGHBRED WORLD CHAMPIONSHIP IN 2017

Old racecourses tend to disappear more frequently than new ones are opened, so it was a refreshing change to see Bro Park being built from scratch on farmland at the top end of Stockholm County.

Bro Park replaced Täby, the traditional home of Swedish racing which was far closer to the capital but sold to developers. Organisers Svensk Gallop have created a well-appointed venue in its place, with a neat main grandstand including wooden features straight out of a Scandi design catalogue. Trainers have relocated to purpose-built stabling just across the road.

Competition tends to include frequent visitors from Norway and Denmark, with the course inheriting a few stakes races headed by the Stockholm Cup, whose history dates back to 1937.

Spectator numbers are not high at Bro Park, and middle-of-the-day fixtures are really just fodder for the betting industry. Summer twilight meetings are more popular and sometimes attract a very famous regular in Benny Andersson, a founder member of ABBA. He has owned and bred horses around Europe and casts a benevolent eye upon the domestic scene.

Jägersro
Sweden

LOCATION: THREE MILES (4.8KM) SOUTHEAST OF CENTRAL MALMÖ

THE TRACK: LEFT-HANDED, FLAT, OVAL, DIRT TRACK OF SEVEN FURLONGS (1,400M); MEETINGS BETWEEN APRIL AND DECEMBER

PRINCIPAL RACES: PRAMMS MEMORIAL, MAY; SWEDISH DERBY, JULY/AUGUST

OPENED: 1907

FAMOUS MOMENTS: GROUP CAPTAIN PETER TOWNSEND, THE FAMOUS ROMANTIC INTEREST OF PRINCESS MARGARET, WINS AN INTERNATIONAL AMATEUR RIDERS' RACE IN 1955

Situated in one of the leafier districts of Malmö, Jägersro racecourse is by some way the most venerable of Sweden's three main racecourses. How things have changed since racing was first staged there: there was no betting – with a ban on the totalisator lasting until 1923 – and it was on grass, around a right-handed course. In 1980, the surface was replaced, and the decision taken to race in the opposite direction.

Jägersro is now a conventional dirt track with decent facilities, including a large glass-fronted restaurant and plenty of indoor and outdoor seating. The most prestigious meetings are staged outside the deep northern winter.

Several cards through the summer offer significant prizes, and the Pramms Memorial in late May, a mile-race for all-aged horses named in honour of owner-breeder Per-Erik Pramm, has been regularly won by British and French visitors. Gay Kelleway, the first female jockey to ride a winner at Royal Ascot in 1987, was also a pioneer in challenging for the Pramms Memorial after becoming a trainer. She brought Vortex, a specialist on the British all-weather

circuit, which scrambled home in 2004 by a head. Vortex returned and ran in the race several times more, in between his visits to Japan and Hollywood Park in California. Premio Loco, another who was campaigned boldly by his trainer, Chris Wall – based like the Kelleway team at Newmarket – plundered the 2012 staging and is probably as good a horse as has run in it.

The Swedish Derby, held in July or August, is more of a domestic affair between the best Scandinavian three-year-olds, and, since its inception in 1918, has been a notable hat-wearing social occasion. Trotting is more popular with Swedish bettors, and some of its feature events, such as the Hugo Åbergs Memorial and the Swedish Trotting Derby, are worth considerably more, and have more status, than the thoroughbred events.

Jägersro is not only a racecourse but also a busy equine centre. There is a city riding school, veterinary clinic and an all-weather exercise track used by around 250 horses, all of which were part of a major new investment in 2008. Even during a big freeze, staff manage to keep the show on the road.

St Moritz

Switzerland

LOCATION: ON THE FROZEN LAKE AT ST MORITZ, 124 MILES (200KM)
SOUTHEAST OF ZURICH, CLOSE TO THE ITALIAN BORDER

THE TRACK: RIGHT-HANDED, TIGHT, FIVE AND A HALF FURLONGS (1,100M)

PRINCIPAL RACES: GROSSER PREIS VON ST MORITZ, FEBRUARY

OPENED: 1907

With its breathtaking Alpine scenery, clean air and almost daily sunshine, it is said that winter tourism was invented at St Moritz in the late 1800s, and for over a century it has staged one of horseracing's most remarkable events as part of all that. It is hard to think where else jockeys would don ski masks, horses wear shoes with special grips and spectators an array of fur; but for the racing that takes place on the frozen lake at St Moritz, all are essentials.

The lake is frozen to an average depth of one and a half feet (50cm) from November/December until the spring, and in February it plays host to the famous 'White Turf'. During the month, crowds of approaching 40,000, dressed to resist the freezing temperatures, pour into the chic resort – home to the Cresta Run – for three racing fixtures, all held on Sundays. The racecard normally contains seven races: four on the flat – ranging from six and a half to nine furlongs (1,300m–1,800m) – two for trotters over eight and a half furlongs (1,700m), and the skijoring event over thirteen and a half furlongs (2,700m).

Alongside the temporary paddock and stands, a tent city including betting area, bars and restaurants is constructed. A course is laid out on a thick layer of packed snow for the Flat racing, trotting and skijoring, where 'jockeys' on skis steer as they are towed along at high speeds, like water-skiers. A white cloud of snow dust follows the runners and riders, both of which have the added hazard of a ferocious 'kick-back', so obtaining and retaining a prominent position during races has its obvious advantages.

Horses have specially designed shoes, with extra grips, to be able to race safely on the snow. Races have been cancelled because the ice is not sufficiently solid or when a serious accident occurs, as in 2017. A three-horse pile-up resulted in the severe head injuries received by the British Classic-winning jockey George Baker, putting an end to his 1,350-plus winner career; Baker's mount Boomerang Bob died.

A hole that had appeared in the ice was blamed for the accident. Under some pressure, officials promised to review all safety measures. A thermal imaging camera mounted on a drone is now used to swoop over the course and detect any possibility of the ice thinning to dangerous levels beneath the snow: modern technology ensuring the immediate future of this most traditional of racing events.

Veliefendi

Turkey

LOCATION: SEVEN MILES (11.3KM) WEST OF CENTRAL ISTANBUL, CLOSE TO THE SEA OF MARMARA

THE TRACK: RIGHT-HANDED, OVAL, TURF OF A MILE AND A QUARTER (2,020M) WITH ARTIFICIAL CIRCUIT INSIDE; RACES ON WEDNESDAYS AND SATURDAYS MOST OF THE YEAR

PRINCIPAL RACES: GAZI RACE, JUNE; BOSPHORUS CUP, TOPKAPI TROPHY, BOTH SEPTEMBER

OPENED: 1913

Turkey might not always have been renowned as a Premier League racing jurisdiction, but it is certainly a country with a keen interest in the horses and a burgeoning scene. Among nine well-appointed tracks, Veliefendi is very much its Ascot or Flemington, hosting most of the important prizes.

The track was constructed when part of the Ottoman Empire, under the instruction of the military leader Enver Pasha, and it thrived when racing became more organised under the regime of Gazi Mustafa Kemal Atatürk in the modern Turkey. The country's most prestigious event, the Gazi Race, was named in his honour and is essentially the Turkish Derby. Atatürk would watch it when in Ankara, its original location before transfer to Veliefendi in 1968. It is hugely valuable and is a real occasion for dressing up.

They take their sport seriously here; after a race in 1949 which punters suspected was rigged, they burned down the grandstands. It was quickly rebuilt and today is modern and comfortable, with many spectators also making use of abundant facilities for picnics in what is now a green area surrounded by high-rise development. There is a giant television screen, a museum and an apprentice school, as well as a large stabling facility.

Turkish racing was enjoyed by visiting gentry but remained something of an internal affair until 1990, and the development of the International Racing Festival each September opening it up to all-comers.

Prize money for what are now internationally recognised Group races are high – far in excess of some other European countries – and the Bosphorus Cup and Topkapi Trophy have been targeted and won on an almost annual basis by British horses from stables including those of Godolphin, Luca Cumani and Richard Hannon.

Most of the local horses are imported but there have been attempts to improve the breeding, driven by racing figures like industrialist Ibrahim Araci, who also keeps horses in Ireland and Britain. His red, white and black-coloured silks are seen frequently on Turkish racecourses. Mehmet Kurt, another powerful businessman, as well as an owner-breeder, won the Turkish Derby twice in the 1990s but latterly he has invested more time into developing a mechanised training system, building the prototype on his farm in Turkey before producing a second version, in the UK, at Lambourn in Berkshire.

Aintree

United Kingdom

LOCATION: IN THE NORTH LIVERPOOL SUBURB OF AINTREE, ABOUT SIX MILES (9.7KM) FROM THE CITY CENTRE

THE TRACK: LEFT-HANDED, TURF; THE GRAND NATIONAL COURSE IS TRIANGULAR, TWO AND A QUARTER MILES (3,620M); THE MILDMAY COURSE IS RECTANGULAR, ONE AND A HALF MILES (2,400M); NATIONAL HUNT ONLY (ALSO FLAT UNTIL 1976), OCTOBER–JUNE

PRINCIPAL RACES: GRAND NATIONAL, APRIL

OPENED: 1829

FAMOUS MOMENTS: RED RUM COMPLETES GRAND NATIONAL TREBLE, 1977

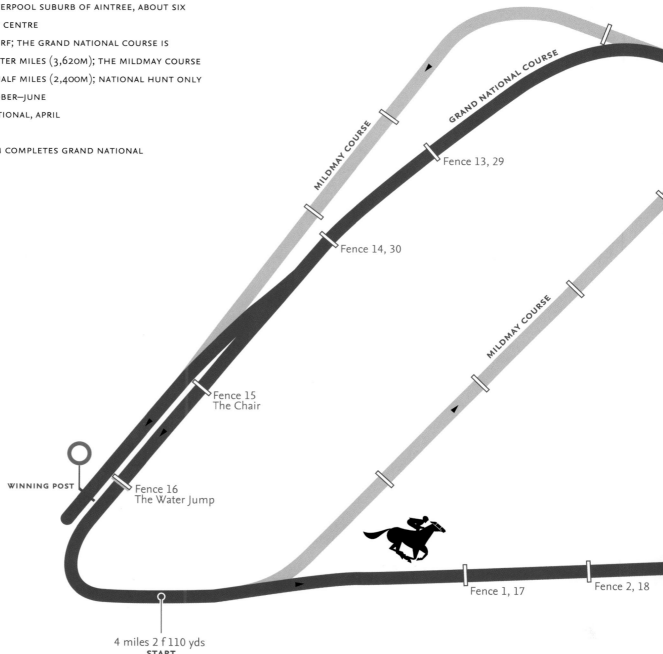

MILDMAY COURSE

GRAND NATIONAL COURSE

Fence 13, 29

Fence 14, 30

MILDMAY COURSE

Fence 15
The Chair

WINNING POST

Fence 16
The Water Jump

Fence 1, 17

Fence 2, 18

4 miles 2 f 110 yds
START
GRAND NATIONAL

NUMBERED FENCES ARE THOSE OF THE GRAND NATIONAL:

BECHER'S BROOK:	FENCES 6 & 22	NAMED AFTER CAPTAIN MARTIN BECHER, WHO FELL AT THIS FENCE AND LANDED IN THE WATER
FOINAVON:	FENCES 7 & 23	NAMED AFTER THE 1967 WINNER OF THE RACE
THE CANAL TURN:	FENCES 8 & 24	90 DEGREE TURN IN THE TRACK IMMEDIATELY AFTER LANDING FROM THE FENCE TO RUN PARALLEL TO THE CANAL
VALENTINE'S BROOK:	FENCES 9 & 25	NAMED AFTER A COMPETING HORSE FROM 1840 THAT WAS RUMOURED TO HAVE JUMPED HIND LEGS FIRST
THE CHAIR:	FENCE 15	THE TALLEST AND BROADEST OF JUMPS IN THE RACE
THE WATER JUMP:	FENCE 16	THE SMALLEST FENCE AT 2FT 9 INCHES

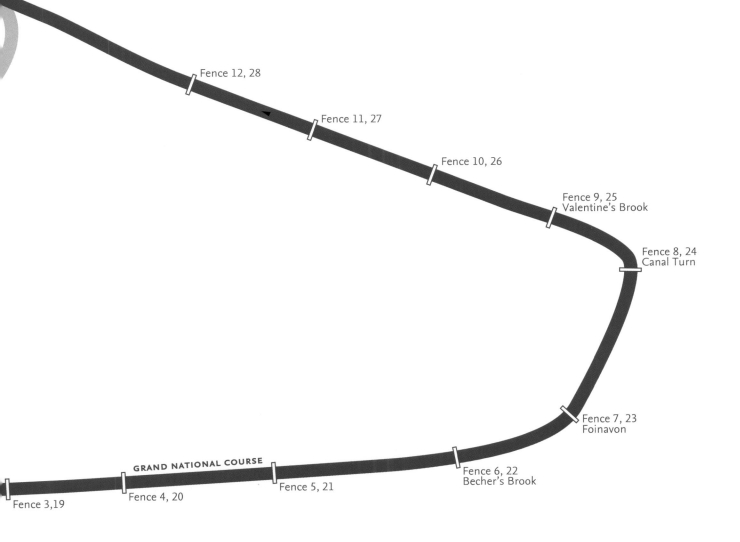

Fence 12, 28

Fence 11, 27

Fence 10, 26

Fence 9, 25
Valentine's Brook

Fence 8, 24
Canal Turn

Fence 7, 23
Foinavon

GRAND NATIONAL COURSE

Fence 5, 21

Fence 6, 22
Becher's Brook

Fence 4, 20

Fence 3,19

Only five races a year are staged over the Grand National course at Aintree; however, with the participants required to clear a series of unique obstacles, some of them amongst the most iconic landmarks in sport, the impression is sometimes taken that they are the only prizes raced for at Aintree.

It has certainly come a long way since the 1820s, when local innkeeper and entrepreneur William Lynn first leased a site for horseracing in the village of Aintree from Lord Sefton.

Exactly how the Grand National took shape in those early years is the subject of debate, but the Grand Liverpool Steeplechase of 1839 has long been recognised as the first. That it was won by a horse named Lottery set the tone for so many of the years ahead, as the race became the ultimate examination of horse and rider, testing abilities of jumping, stamina and horsemanship over two circuits of the course and thirty fences.

Probably the most sensational staging of the race was in 1967, when Foinavon, a 100-1 no-hoper, was so far behind a pile-up of twenty-seven runners caused by a loose horse at the fence that subsequently bore his name that his jockey John Buckingham was able to safely navigate a path through the tangled chaos.

Although Foinavon and Buckingham went clear by a furlong or more, many of their rivals still set off in pursuit, but the fortunate duo still had fifteen lengths to spare over Honey End at the winning line. To this day in British racing circles, you'll hear people say that such and such an event was the 'biggest shock since Foinavon' despite there having been other 100-1 winners.

While the regular thrills and spills of horseracing were to the fore in Foinavon's year, no one can fully explain the events of 1956. Devon Loch, owned by Queen Elizabeth the Queen Mother and ridden by Dick Francis, seemed home for all money when he effectively belly-flopped onto the turf near the finish, presenting the race to E.S.B. Francis, later a successful thriller writer, speculated that perhaps the horse 'saw' the shape of a fence that was not there, and made to jump it.

The run from the final fence past 'the Elbow' to the race's end has witnessed many changes in fortune. None was greater than

in 1973 when the ex-Australian chaser Crisp, clear of his rivals for much of the race, was run down by Red Rum in the final strides. 'Rummy' and the irrepressible Donald 'Ginger' McCain, who trained the horse on the beach at nearby Southport, became household names during the 1970s. Red Rum recorded a historic Grand National treble in 1973, 1974 and 1977, and took the runners-up spot in between.

In 2004, McCain equalled the big-race records of trainers George Dockeray and Fred Rimell by claiming a fourth trophy with Amberleigh House; seven years later, his son, Donald junior, also took the race with Ballabriggs. One of the Grand National's – British sport's – greatest fairy stories came in 1981 when jockey Bob Champion, who had overcome cancer, won the race on Aldaniti, a horse only just back in action following a career-threatening leg injury.

Other notable winners include Manifesto (1897 and 1899), who participated on a record eight occasions; Golden Miller (1934), the only horse to complete the Cheltenham Gold Cup–Grand National double in the same year; and Don't Push It (2010), who brought success at the fifteenth attempt to jockey Sir A.P. McCoy.

There was no winner in 1993 when the race was declared void and all betting stakes returned after a series of false starts; in 1997 the race, in which Lord Gyllene was victorious, was delayed 48 hours by a bomb scare.

Aintree's reputation as a daunting challenge has brought with it controversy following deaths and injuries to horses. In 2012, officials received widespread support for modifications to the course, which were designed to improve safety while retaining the race's character. Without that, the future of one of sport's most historic institutions had looked uncertain.

Uncertainty had also prevailed during the 1970s and 1980s when the course's position in 270 acres on the edge of Liverpool brought the threat of closure and development for housing. Its popularity had been waning, and Muriel Topham, whose family were long associated with the course and bought the freehold in 1949, developing a Grand Prix circuit in the 1950s, sold to a property developer, Bill Davies. Bookmakers Ladbrokes managed to secure a lease for a while, but doubts about the future continued until Aintree was purchased in 1983 by a charitable trust following an appeal for funds.

Down on its nose at Becher's, so to speak, it scrambled to its feet, and can be said to have hardly looked back since.

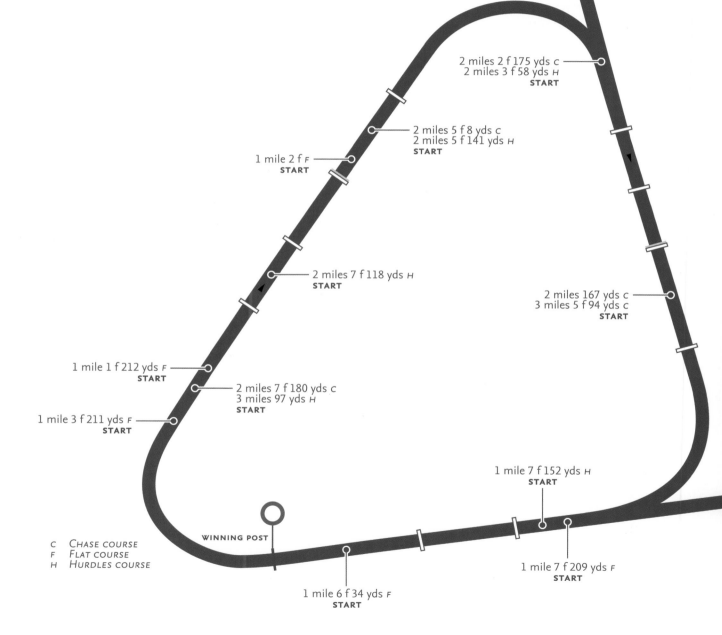

7 furlongs 213 yds *F*
START

2 miles 2 f 175 yds *C*
2 miles 3 f 58 yds *H*
START

2 miles 5 f 8 yds *C*
2 miles 5 f 141 yds *H*
START

1 mile 2 f *F*
START

2 miles 7 f 118 yds *H*
START

2 miles 167 yds *C*
3 miles 5 f 94 yds *C*
START

1 mile 1 f 212 yds *F*
START

2 miles 7 f 180 yds *C*
3 miles 97 yds *H*
START

1 mile 3 f 211 yds *F*
START

1 mile 7 f 152 yds *H*
START

WINNING POST

C   *CHASE COURSE*
F   *FLAT COURSE*
H   *HURDLES COURSE*

1 mile 7 f 209 yds *F*
START

1 mile 6 f 34 yds *F*
START

Ascot

United Kingdom

LOCATION: TWENTY-FIVE MILES (40.2KM) WEST OF CENTRAL LONDON AND SIX MILES (9.7KM) SOUTHWEST OF WINDSOR CASTLE

THE TRACK: UNDULATING AND EXAMINING, RIGHT-HANDED, ROUGHLY TRIANGULAR TRACK WITH ADDITIONAL STRAIGHT COURSE; TURF COURSE OF ABOUT A MILE AND THREE-QUARTERS (2,816M), THREE-FURLONG (600M) HOME STRAIGHT; FLAT RACING APRIL–OCTOBER, NATIONAL HUNT OCTOBER–MARCH

PRINCIPAL RACES: ROYAL ASCOT, JUNE; KING GEORGE ETC, JULY; BRITISH CHAMPIONS DAY, OCTOBER

OPENED: 1711

FAMOUS MOMENTS: SINCE 1825, THE ROYAL PARTY HAS ARRIVED FOR THE ROYAL MEETING IN A CARRIAGE PROCESSION

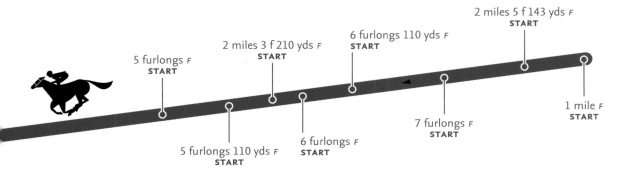

5 furlongs F START

5 furlongs 110 yds F START

2 miles 3 f 210 yds F START

6 furlongs F START

6 furlongs 110 yds F START

7 furlongs F START

2 miles 5 f 143 yds F START

1 mile F START

All the pomp and ceremony of royal connections – dating back more than three hundred years – mixed with Europe's outstanding festival of Flat racing ensures Royal Ascot and the course on which it takes place occupies a singular position on the sporting stage.

It was in the early summer of 1711 that Queen Anne is said to have discovered a heath near Windsor Castle which she thought ideal for racing. The Master of the Royal Buckhounds was instructed to have the area cleared of scrub and gorse for a race meeting for hunting-horses that August.

In 1749, four days of racing took place, a format that remained for more than 250 years until a fifth was added to mark the Queen's Golden Jubilee of 2002, while from 1766 the meeting began to take place, as now, in June; until 1946 it was the sole fixture.

Since those early days, the royal link has been maintained, and in the 1820s, George IV started an exclusive area for himself and his friends, which would develop into the Royal Enclosure. George also began the tradition of the formal procession, and to this day the arrival of the Royals in open-topped landaus, manned by liveried staff and pulled by Windsor grey and bay horses, is one of the highlights of the British summer social calendar. Edward VII revelled in the week, and when his death occurred not long before 1910's Royal Ascot a rapid change of dress code to black was ordered.

Queen Elizabeth II became the first reigning monarch to own a horse that won the Gold Cup – the historic centrepiece since 1807 – when Estimate was successful in 2013. The two-and-a-half-mile (4,000m) Gold Cup takes place on day three of the Tuesday-to-Saturday Royal Ascot programme – 'Ladies Day', a description first referred to in 1823, and the backdrop to the iconic 'Ascot Gavotte' scene in *My Fair Lady*.

While for purists, the horses are the number one attraction, for many others attendance is more of a social outing, with the priority being visits to bars or restaurants and taking part in the traditional post-racing singing at the bandstand. And although attitudes have moved with the times to an extent, expectations about standards of dress, particularly in the Royal Enclosure, remain high. Men in the Royal Enclosure must wear the black or grey morning suits with waistcoats and top hats that have been traditional since the days of George IV; for women, dresses or skirts are required to be of a 'modest length', just above the knee or longer. Although, looking around, it is clear few reminders are required, headwear is also insisted upon. For many years, a recommendation was required for admission into the Royal Enclosure, and until 1955 divorcees were not welcome. These days, 300,000 or so racegoers crowd in, generally seeming to enjoy the more quaint or old-fashioned-sounding rules and regulations.

A £220 million replacement of the dull-looking, but much-loved, 1960s stand and other facilities between 2004 and 2006 – during which the Royal meeting was staged at York – did not, initially, go down well with all, particularly with traditionalists. The vast, state-of-the-art grandstand was not popular, nor were some of the new viewing angles; the moving of the paddock and winners' enclosure to positions behind the stand was lamented; and the effect on the going created by alterations to the straight course was criticised. However, after just a few years of getting used to the changes, plus some adjustments by managers, most critics went silent.

In contrast, no one is complaining about the quality of the racing, which no longer principally revolves around the premier Flat racers from Britain, Ireland and France; a drive from the mid-1990s to encourage contenders from further afield has paid dividends, with the lure of Royal Ascot too much to resist for international runners, notably from Australia and America.

Away from the Royal meeting, the addition to Ascot's fixture list in July of the mile-and-a-half-long (2,400m), all-aged King George VI and Queen Elizabeth Stakes in 1951 proved highly significant. A long list of high-quality winners includes Grundy, after a compelling duel with Bustino in 1975, often rated the 'race of the century'.

The Shergar Cup challenge for home and overseas jockeys every August has been a notable success, while the course benefitted from a radical shake-up of British racing's end-of-season programme from October 2011 when, to take advantage of 'brand Ascot', Champions Day, the richest racecard of the season, was relocated from Newmarket.

It was at Ascot's previous autumn highlight, the Festival of British Racing, that in 1996 jockey Frankie Dettori won all seven races – a towering achievement on such a stellar day – at combined starting-price odds of 25,095-1. This time, it was 'jockey royalty' that was making the headlines.

Cheltenham

United Kingdom

LOCATION: ON THE NORTHERN EDGE OF THE GLOUCESTERSHIRE
TOWN OF CHELTENHAM

THE TRACK: LEFT-HANDED; THREE COURSES — OLD: OVAL, ONE AND A HALF
MILES (2,400M), 350-YARD (320M) RUN-IN; NEW: OVAL, ONE MILE AND
FIVE FURLONGS (2,600M), 220-YARD (200M) RUN-IN; CROSS COUNTRY;
RACING OCTOBER—MAY

PRINCIPAL RACES: GOLD CUP, CHAMPION HURDLE,
QUEEN MOTHER CHAMPION CHASE, ALL MARCH

OPENED: 1898

FAMOUS MOMENTS: ARKLE COMPLETES GOLD CUP HAT-TRICK, 1966

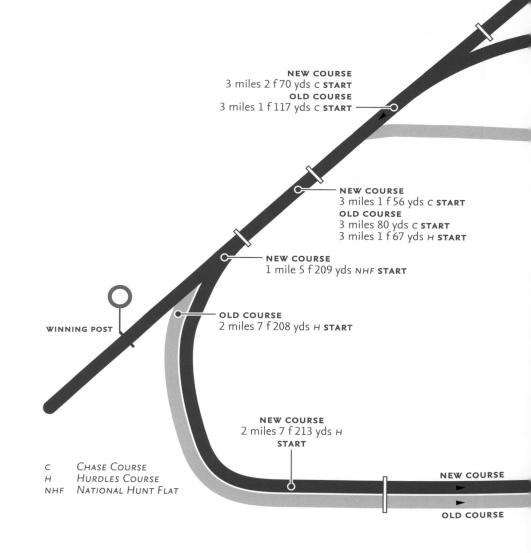

NEW COURSE
3 miles 2 f 70 yds C **START**
OLD COURSE
3 miles 1 f 117 yds C **START**

NEW COURSE
3 miles 1 f 56 yds C **START**
OLD COURSE
3 miles 80 yds C **START**
3 miles 1 f 67 yds H **START**

NEW COURSE
1 mile 5 f 209 yds NHF **START**

OLD COURSE
2 miles 7 f 208 yds H **START**

WINNING POST

NEW COURSE
2 miles 7 f 213 yds H
START

C   *CHASE COURSE*
H   *HURDLES COURSE*
NHF   *NATIONAL HUNT FLAT*

NEW COURSE

OLD COURSE

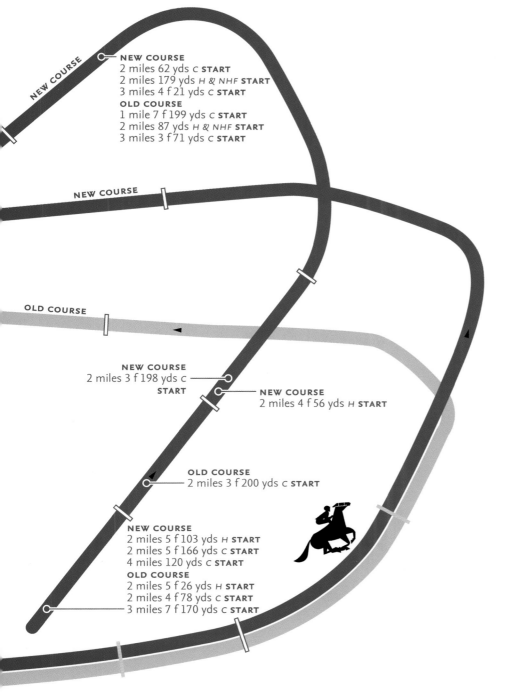

NEW COURSE
2 miles 62 yds *C* **START**
2 miles 179 yds *H & NHF* **START**
3 miles 4 f 21 yds *C* **START**
OLD COURSE
1 mile 7 f 199 yds *C* **START**
2 miles 87 yds *H & NHF* **START**
3 miles 3 f 71 yds *C* **START**

NEW COURSE

OLD COURSE

NEW COURSE
2 miles 3 f 198 yds *C*
START

NEW COURSE
2 miles 4 f 56 yds *H* **START**

OLD COURSE
2 miles 3 f 200 yds *C* **START**

NEW COURSE
2 miles 5 f 103 yds *H* **START**
2 miles 5 f 166 yds *C* **START**
4 miles 120 yds *C* **START**
OLD COURSE
2 miles 5 f 26 yds *H* **START**
2 miles 4 f 78 yds *C* **START**
3 miles 7 f 170 yds *C* **START**

Few, if any, sports have a spiritual home that to its supporters is as iconic as Cheltenham is for National Hunt racing. This is the place where practically all of jumping's biggest names – human and equine – have been crowned and celebrated, principally at the four-day National Hunt Festival in March. And it is not just about the star players; it is about the location too. Positioned in a natural amphitheatre, below the rolling Cotswold Hills, it looks almost as though it was intentionally constructed for horseracing. For an enthusiast, a day at Cheltenham, with Cleeve Hill rising to nearly 1,100 feet (330m) above, and glowing in any sunshine, is its own pinnacle.

Racing has taken place in the Cheltenham area since the early nineteenth century when the restorative reputation of the spa town's waters was ever-burgeoning. In 1818, a meeting of five Flat races was organised on Cleeve Hill; with popularity soaring, a large viewing stand was built, apparently visible for miles around, and in 1825 as many as 50,000 people are said to have attended. However, a fiery local parson, Francis Close, preached effectively against the evils of racing and gambling, and in 1830 the stand was burnt down by arsonists.

Today's location at Prestbury Park then came into use for Flat races, while steeplechasing, featuring the Grand Annual Chase, was taking place at Andoversford, on the road to Oxford. In the years around the turn of the twentieth century, the jump racing transferred to Prestbury Park, and in 1911 the previously movable feast that was the 'National Hunt Meeting' – forerunner to the Cheltenham Festival – was established on a permanent basis.

Familiar race names like the National Hunt Chase and Grand Annual Chase were quickly part of the programme, but it was not until the 1920s that the most prestigious trophies of today were introduced: the Gold Cup in 1924 and the Champion Hurdle three years later. The Champion Two-Mile Chase came along in 1959, later being renamed the Queen Mother Champion Chase in 1980 to mark the 80th birthday of Queen Elizabeth, a long-term jump racing and Festival devotee. The Stayers Hurdle with its current name started in 1972.

A new stand had been constructed for 1911, and further works followed through the decades: the main grandstand was completed in 1979, and the vast £45 million, sandy-coloured Princess Royal Stand fitted in well when it was opened in 2015. On the track, horses must be able to gallop and jump uphill and down, be agile enough to avoid being caught out at the downhill third last fence and have the stamina to last home up an examining final hill.

Golden Miller put the Gold Cup on the map, winning on a record five occasions during the 1930s, and in 1934 becoming the only horse to complete the Gold Cup–Grand National double in the same season. After the Second World War, the tradition of Ireland sending its best jumpers to Cheltenham grew, with hat-tricks by Cottage Rake in the Gold Cup (1948–1950) and Champion Hurdler Hatton's Grace (1949–1951), ushering in a dominant period for their trainer Vincent O'Brien.

In the 1960s, the peerless Arkle was travelled from Ireland to carry off the Gold Cup three times, ridden by Pat Taaffe, between 1964 and 1966, twice defeating British star Mill House. Arkle – 'Himself' – is revered as probably National Hunt racing's greatest horse, and is remembered at the course with a race at the Festival, a statue and a bar.

Irish-trained horses reached further notable historic peaks when the charismatic pairing of Dawn Run and jockey Jonjo O'Neill recorded success in the 1986 Gold Cup two years after they had won the Champion Hurdle; and from 1998 to 2000, Istabraq – owned like many other winners at Cheltenham by the gambler JP McManus – won three successive Champion Hurdles.

There have been disappointing years too, though numbers of Irish punters and Guinness sales hardly faltered. But with some big-money backers concentrated in Ireland, the stables of two highly skilled trainers in Willie Mullins – many of whose horses are ridden by Cheltenham-favourite jockey Ruby Walsh – and Gordon Elliott have been in the ascendancy.

In the 1960s and 1970s – when names like Persian War, Bula, Comedy Of Errors, Night Nurse, Monksfield and Sea Pigeon ensured a golden era for hurdling – the on-track attendance for what was a three-day Festival hovered around the 70,000 mark. There were similar numbers when trainer Michael Dickinson pulled off a barely credible 1-2-3-4-5 headed by Bregawn in 1983.

Growth towards the major British sporting event of today received a significant boost from the Gold Cup victory of the popular 'flying grey' Desert Orchid in 1989; more recently the Gold Cup success of Best Mate and big-race rivalry between Kauto Star and Denman plus the exploits of Sprinter Sacre and Cue Card have only served to raise the profile further.

In 2018, staged over four days, this once parochial event – in terms of the jump racing parish – attracted an on-course crowd of more than 260,000, many wearing the tweed for which Cheltenham racegoers are renowned. Away from the course, millions more were following on radio, TV, online and in high-street betting shops.

The week is believed to have given the extended Cotswold economy a boost of around £100 million, and betting on the twenty-eight races has exceeded £300 million; little wonder the gloom extended further than simply National Hunt ranks when foot-and-mouth disease forced cancellation in 2001.

There are, of course, a whole lot of other successful Cheltenham fixtures, notably the three afternoons of the Open meeting in November and on New Year's Day, but it is around the Festival that everything – the whole sport indeed – revolves.

Passing Dean Close School on the way out of Cheltenham, it is hard not to think about the Reverend Francis spinning in his grave.

Chester

United Kingdom

LOCATION: ON THE ROODEE, BELOW THE CITY WALLS, A SHORT WALK FROM THE CITY CENTRE

THE TRACK: LEFT-HANDED, TURF, ONE MILE AND 73 YARDS (1,676M) ROUND, 230-YARD (210M) HOME STRAIGHT

PRINCIPAL RACES: CHESTER CUP, CHESTER VASE, CHESHIRE OAKS, ALL IN MAY

OPENED: 1539

The Roodee racecourse at Chester is Britain's smallest track, squeezed in between the city's ancient walls – which remain a popular, free vantage point – the river Dee and a railway viaduct. This all creates something of an amphitheatre feel, recalling the days when Chester was a Roman settlement, especially as the fifteen or so racing days a year regularly attract crowds of up to 40,000; nowhere can spectators get closer to the action.

The weighing room and paddock are in the centre of the course, with access via a subway from the main enclosures on the outside. The runners are always 'on the turn', so an inside draw in the starting stalls is deemed highly desirable, especially in races over the minimum five-furlong (1,000m) distance. Indeed, part of the reason for the tightening of rules concerning late withdrawals of runners was in response to so many horses being scratched at Chester after being allotted wide berths. Equally, diners at racing parties where the company has proved disappointing have been known to say they felt as though they had been 'drawn eighteen at Chester'.

The Roodee is not only the smallest racecourse in Britain, but also the oldest, having basically always stayed put, with a just a couple of breaks for the Civil War and disagreements amongst locals. The first race held there, on Shrove Tuesday in 1539, was started by a mayor named Henry Gee – possibly the origin of the expression 'gee-gees' – after an annual free-for-all with a leather football was banned, such was the violence that it had involved.

In the 1800s the track grew markedly in popularity and a stand was added; a much-loved, half-timbered replacement came in 1900, but that was burnt down by arson in 1985.

The turns of the track test a horse's athleticism, and are regarded by trainers as a good place to race potential runners for the Classics staged around the tricky course at Epsom. Derby winners to have graduated from Chester include Shergar (1981) and Ruler Of The World (2013), while the outstanding filly Enable started a prolific big-race run in 2017 – which included the Oaks at Epsom – at Chester.

The first TV pictures ever seen in betting shops were beamed from Chester in May 1987, and although the track has bookmakers, other on-course betting services are run by the track itself under the name 'Chester Bet'.

Doncaster

United Kingdom

LOCATION: ON TOWN MOOR, TWO MILES (3.2KM) FROM THE TOWN CENTRE

THE TRACK: LEFT-HANDED, PEAR-SHAPED, LEVEL; FLAT AND NATIONAL HUNT; CIRCUIT OF ONE MILE, SEVEN FURLONGS AND 110 YARDS (3,118M); A LITTLE OVER HALF-A-MILE (920M) HOME STRAIGHT; FLAT SEASON FROM MARCH TO NOVEMBER AND JUMPING SEASON FROM DECEMBER TO EARLY MARCH

PRINCIPAL RACES: ST LEGER, SEPTEMBER; RACING POST TROPHY, OCTOBER

OPENED: PRE-1600

'At Doncaster,' wrote the American writer Benjamin Silliman in his travel journals of 1805–06, 'I observed the extensive race grounds for one of the favourite amusements of the English. There is also a large building which serves as a kind of office or stand for the gamblers of the turf who are very numerous in Yorkshire.' And so they continue to be, demonstrating enthusiasm aplenty, particularly at Doncaster; the buzz of pride generated by the St Leger, Flat racing's oldest Classic prize, is positively infectious. They even give life membership of the course to the first St Leger Day baby born in the town.

With a sandy soil, 'Donny' stages an all-year-round programme. The Flat season starts with the Lincoln Handicap – transferred from the defunct Lincoln in 1965 – and continues until the November Handicap, itself moved on Manchester's closure in 1964. Moving things about has become something of a habit, with the St Leger also staged variously at Newmarket, Manchester, Thirsk, York and Ayr, because of war or refurbishment or, in Ayr's case, following the discovery of a hole in the Doncaster turf.

The St Leger had a somewhat anonymous start on Doncaster's Cantley Common in 1776; the then two-mile (3,200m) race had not yet received its famous title, and the five or six runners – records are unclear exactly which – were not named at the time (as was not completely compulsory until 1946). The winner was a filly owned by the two-time British prime minister, the Marquess of Rockingham, who subsequently named her Allabaculia. Two years later, the race became the St Leger, then pronounced 'Sell-in-jer', after Anthony St Leger, one of the co-founders.

Although the third part of Flat racing's Triple Crown, staged since 1826 over a mile and three-quarters plus 132 yards (2,937m), it rather lost its sheen during the 1960s and 1970s. This was not least because the iconic 1970 Triple Crown winner Nijinsky, one of eight St Leger successes ridden by Lester Piggott, was beaten in that season's Prix de l'Arc de Triomphe. However, with the backing of prominent owners, trainers and the Arena Racing Company as owner-manager, it has climbed back, and pictures of the winning rider in a traditional if somewhat oversized replica jockey's cap seem to be making newspaper front pages again.

In 1992 the course staged the first Sunday racing in Britain – albeit, at that stage, without any betting – while it was at Doncaster in 2017 that Aidan O'Brien broke the world record for victories-trained at Group or Grade One level in a calendar year (25) when Saxon Warrior was successful in the Racing Post Trophy – he went on to saddle two more.

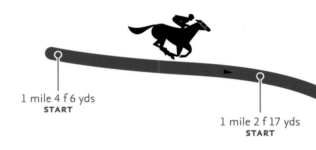

1 mile 4 f 6 yds
START

1 mile 2 f 17 yds
START

1 mile 113 yds
START

Epsom

United Kingdom

LOCATION: ON THE SURREY DOWNS AT EPSOM, FOURTEEN MILES (22.5KM) SOUTHWEST OF BIG BEN IN CENTRAL LONDON

THE TRACK: STEEP IN PLACES, LEFT-HANDED, HORSESHOE WITH CHUTES, TURF, A MILE AND A HALF (2,400M) IN LENGTH, HOME STRAIGHT OF JUST UNDER A HALF-MILE (800M); RACING APRIL–SEPTEMBER

PRINCIPAL RACES: THE DERBY, OAKS AND CORONATION CUP, ALL JUNE

OPENED: 1700

FAMOUS MOMENTS: THE INFAMOUS SUFFRAGETTE DERBY OF 1913, WHEN EMILY DAVISON WALKED INTO THE PATH OF THE KING'S HORSE ANMER

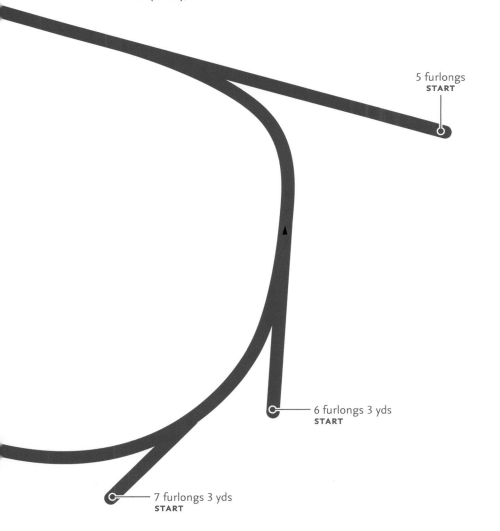

5 furlongs
START

6 furlongs 3 yds
START

7 furlongs 3 yds
START

Although they call Newmarket Flat racing's 'headquarters', it is not hard to argue that the racecourse on the Surrey Downs at Epsom is the more influential. Since Sir Charles Bunbury's Diomed won the first Derby in 1780 – one year after Lord Derby's filly Bridget was successful in the Oaks for fillies over the same course – the race's name, one-and-a-half-mile (2,400m) distance and three-year-olds-only format has been emulated all around the world.

It is said that the toss of a coin or perhaps the drawing of straw lots between Bunbury and Derby decided the name of the new race. Originally staged over one mile (1,600m), the distance was soon increased by half again, and in 1872 the famous horseshoe-shaped course in use today replaced previous locations on the Downs.

It is one of the more eccentric layouts of any racetrack in the world, but consequently a true test of athleticism, speed and stamina as well as class. On the Derby course, the runners race uphill to halfway, a point which is 142 feet (43m) higher than where they started; they then turn left and soon start the sharp descent down to, around and beyond the Tattenham Corner landmark. They are further tested by a tricky camber through much of the closing stages; it provides a unique examination which has for centuries regularly singled out the best, and future outstanding stallions and broodmares.

As the distinguished Italian breeder Federico Tesio once said: 'The thoroughbred exists because its selection has depended, not on experts, technicians or zoologists, but on a piece of wood: the winning post of the Epsom Derby.'

The course's unique gradients make the downhill five-furlong (1,000m) sprint course, starting on a chute, the fastest in the world.

With Epsom's close proximity to London and the already established popularity of the apparent healing powers of its salts, the Derby did not take long to catch the public imagination. It grew also as a training centre. Derby Day became the great London day out, with shops, offices and even Parliament closing to allow people to attend. In 1793, *The Times* wrote of the road to Epsom being full of crowds 'hurtling to the races; some to plunder and some to be plundered. Horses, gigs, curricles, coaches, chaises, carts and pedestrians covered the Downs'.

Nothing much has changed: the traffic remains heavy – in 1971, the trainer Ian Balding was forced to sprint the final mile to saddle the winner Mill Reef after getting stuck in a jam – and the crowds still spread across the common land of the Downs, albeit more thinly. Although bare-knuckle boxers and fighting cocks may be a thing of the past, just as red double-decker buses have replaced horse-drawn coaches, it is not hard to identify the modern equivalent of the 'musicians, clowns and coconut stalls' Charles Dickens described in the 1850s.

No bigger act of 'plundering' took place than in 1844 when it emerged that the first horse home, Running Rein, was in fact a four-year-old 'ringer', Maccabeus. The plot, which involved using black hair dye to make the two appear identical, ended up in court with the runner-up Orlando being awarded the race and the conspirators fleeing abroad.

Royalty has been an almost perennial supporter. King Edward VII became the first reigning monarch to win, with Minoru in 1909, and it was in the silks of Edward's son, King George V, that jockey Herbert Jones was riding Anmer in what became known as the Suffragette Derby of 1913. The activist Emily Wilding Davison was hit by Anmer when she walked out in front of the runners at Tattenham Corner; she died of her injuries, but it remains unclear if she intended to kill herself or was making an ill-fated attempt to throw a flag at the royal runner.

In 1953, only a few days after the Coronation, the Queen watched her horse Aureole finish Derby runner-up behind Pinza, ridden by the champion jockey Sir Gordon Richards, having his twenty-eighth attempt at winning. Probably the race's most striking success in the modern era was that achieved by Shergar when he won by ten lengths in 1981. The colt, later kidnapped before disappearing, won by so far that BBC radio's commentator Peter Bromley declared that 'you need a telescope to see the rest'.

Like most stagings from 1838, Shergar's Derby took place on a Wednesday, but in 1995 the decision was made to switch to Saturday. The move did not receive universal approval, and the status of the event was initially affected, however, fortunes have since gone some way to reviving. And, whatever else happens, with the Derby's name and ongoing ability to produce significant winners, the influence of Epsom as its home will remain strong.

Goodwood

United Kingdom

LOCATION: CLOSE TO THE SOUTH COAST OF ENGLAND, FOUR MILES (6.4KM) NORTHEAST OF CHICHESTER
THE TRACK: UNDULATING AND PRINCIPALLY RIGHT-HANDED, L-SHAPED TURF WITH CHUTES AND ABLE TO STAGE RACES OF UP TO TWO AND A HALF MILES (4,000M), HOME STRAIGHTS OF HALF A MILE (800M); RACING MAY–OCTOBER

PRINCIPAL RACES: GOODWOOD CUP, SUSSEX STAKES, STEWARDS CUP, GLORIOUS GOODWOOD, LATE JULY/EARLY AUGUST
OPENED: 1802
FAMOUS MOMENTS: FIRST RACE COMMENTARY ON A BRITISH RACECOURSE, 1952

It is lost in the mists of time quite how Goodwood received its 'Glorious' appendage, but no one is reaching for the Trades Descriptions Act. One of sport's best-known pieces of alliteration – quite likely thought up by a newspaper sub-editor for the headline to a story about King Edward VII and Queen Alexandra, both Goodwood regulars – sums up the racecourse on a good day to perfection.

Set high above the cathedral city of Chichester, on the sprawling, 12,000-acre-plus ancestral estate of the Dukes of Richmond on the Sussex Downs, the scenery does indeed provide a stunning backdrop. The view north from the elegant stands is of a racecourse snaking its way across rolling hills and lush green pastures, while behind, to the south, the sun shimmers on the waters of the Solent in the distance, with the Isle of Wight beyond. Below, but also on the estate, is the motor racing circuit where Goodwood's successful Festival of Speed and Revival events take place.

The racecourse was created in 1802 by the third Duke of Richmond, whose grandfather, an illegitimate son of Charles II, had fallen in love with Goodwood while riding with the prestigious Charlton Hunt. As the high-summer festival now known as 'Glorious Goodwood' became more and more fashionable over the following century, it was Edward VII who described it as a 'garden party with racing tacked on'. The king enjoyed the low-key formality, and it was he who set the trend of wearing a linen suit and Panama

hat, which remains de rigueur for male racegoers. For women, the racecourse's style guide recommends 'an effortless dress that feels fun but chic'. However, in 2007, the eleventh Duke of Richmond, then the Earl of March, criticised the dress standards of some visitors and was forced to defend himself from accusations of snobbishness. The course itself is complex and regularly throws up hard-luck stories. Jockey Richard Hughes was considered a master prior to his retirement in 2015, while Frankie Dettori's initial British winner, Lizzie Hare, was at Goodwood in 1987.

Goodwood's early-season Classic trial races no longer have quite the cachet that once they had, but the Group One features of Glorious Goodwood continue to be important beacons in the Flat racing season. The quality of runner in the historic Goodwood Cup has ensured top-level status; while the mile-long (1,600m) Sussex Stakes, blighted by a string of one-horse 'walkovers' in its early years in the mid-nineteenth century, has more recently been won by star names including Brigadier Gerard, Rock Of Gibraltar and Frankel. The five-day fixture ends with the Stewards Cup handicap, one of Flat racing's biggest-betting and most thrilling-to-watch dashes, as up to twenty-eight runners emerge into sight from a dip in the track, cavalry-like, before thundering up the straight course.

Glorious – most of the time: because the West Sussex weather also knows the definition of 'inglorious', and when the heavens open or a sea fret swirls in, barely anything is visible.

Newmarket

United Kingdom

LOCATION: ON NEWMARKET HEATH ON THE EDGE OF THE TOWN OF
NEWMARKET, SIXTY-FIVE MILES (104.6KM) NORTHEAST OF LONDON

THE TRACK: RIGHT-HANDED, SHAPE OF OPEN GARDEN SHEARS, TURF;
TWO PRINCIPAL COURSES SHARE STRAIGHT BEFORE RIGHT TURN ONTO TOP
'BLADE' (JULY COURSE, STIFF ONE MILE (1,600M), STRAIGHT) OR BOTTOM
'BLADE' (ROWLEY MILE, ONE AND A QUARTER MILES (2,000M), STRAIGHT
WITH SIGNIFICANT DIP THROUGH FINAL FURLONG); RACES ON ROWLEY
MILE APRIL–MAY AND SEPTEMBER–OCTOBER, JULY COURSE JUNE–AUGUST

PRINCIPAL RACES: 2000 GUINEAS AND 1000 GUINEAS, BOTH IN MAY,
DEWHURST STAKES, OCTOBER (ROWLEY MILE); JULY CUP (JULY COURSE)

OPENED: MID-1613

FAMOUS MOMENTS: NUMEROUS, BUT THE BRILLIANT DEFEAT OF BIG
NAMES MILL REEF AND MY SWALLOW BY BRIGADIER GERARD IN THE 1971
2000 GUINEAS RATES HIGHLY

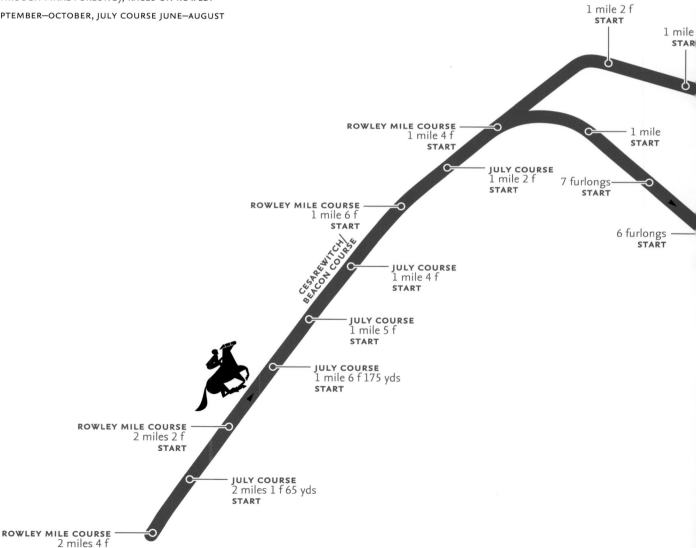

1 mile 2 f
START

1 mile
START

ROWLEY MILE COURSE
1 mile 4 f
START

1 mile
START

JULY COURSE
1 mile 2 f
START

7 furlongs
START

ROWLEY MILE COURSE
1 mile 6 f
START

CESAREWITCH/
BEACON COURSE

JULY COURSE
1 mile 4 f
START

6 furlongs
START

JULY COURSE
1 mile 5 f
START

JULY COURSE
1 mile 6 f 175 yds
START

ROWLEY MILE COURSE
2 miles 2 f
START

JULY COURSE
2 miles 1 f 65 yds
START

ROWLEY MILE COURSE
2 miles 4 f
START

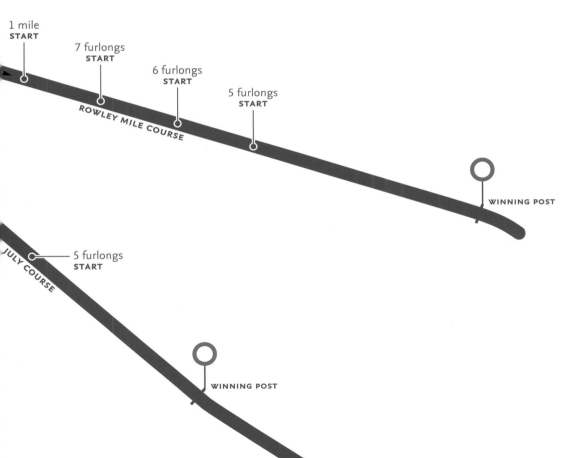

1 mile
START

7 furlongs
START

6 furlongs
START

5 furlongs
START

ROWLEY MILE COURSE

WINNING POST

JULY COURSE

5 furlongs
START

WINNING POST

To many in Flat racing, Newmarket is simply 'Headquarters', a position it has held since the seventeenth century when horseracing became the 'Sport of Kings'. James I built a palace just off the high street and encouraged races between horses owned and ridden by courtiers. His son Charles I was equally enthusiastic. During the Cromwellian years, after Charles I had been held under house-arrest in the town and then tried and executed, racing was banned for being too royalist and potential cover for plotting.

Things took off again after Charles II reclaimed the throne in 1660. During his reign, Charles would spend weeks at a time in Newmarket, and in 1665 created a race that would become the Town Plate – to continue 'for ever' – even marking out the course himself and creating the rules, which became the earliest governing horseracing. In 1671 and 1675, at Newmarket, he became the only British monarch to ride the winner of a recognised horse race. The Town Plate still takes place annually, for total amateur riders, 'no serving man or groom', over its own three-and-three-quarter-mile (6,000m) distance, with a first prize of £200, a trophy and a box of Newmarket sausages.

Successive kings and queens kept up – and indeed keep up – racing's strong tradition of royal patronage, though in the 1790s the Prince of Wales, subsequently King George IV, abandoned Newmarket after his jockey Sam Chifney was accused of skulduggery on a royal runner named Escape. Authorities at the Jockey Club urged the prince to dismiss Chifney or otherwise face the consequence that 'no gentleman would start against him', but he stood by his man.

Formed in 1750, the aristocratic Jockey Club started by running races at Newmarket, often two-horse matches on which there were vast bets; gradually it then took over nationwide regulation, something it maintained until 2006 when the British Horseracing Authority assumed full control. Nowadays, the Jockey Club has an ownership portfolio that includes fifteen racecourses and the training gallops at Newmarket and in Lambourn. As well as the Rowley Mile – taken from Charles II's nickname 'Old Rowley' – and the July Course, the 2,500 acres of Newmarket Heath contain facilities for 3,000 horses in training. Until the early twentieth century, there was also a National Hunt course for jumpers on the site of the Links Golf Club.

The wide-open spaces in which both courses are laid out are done so with the runners rather than spectators in mind. The Town Plate apart, there is no 'round' track, so the runners make their way to starts across the Heath before racing back; famously, October's two-and-a-quarter-mile (3,600m) Cesarewitch Handicap, first staged in 1839, starts in Cambridgeshire and finishes in Suffolk. All that said, both the Rowley Mile and the July Course boast considerably enhanced facilities for racegoers, notably the former's Millennium grandstand opened in 2000.

Many regulars prefer the tree-lined July Course with its thatched administration building, for its very British, church-fete-like summer atmosphere even if it is often accompanied by midges. The three-day July Festival, with the internationally renowned Group One July Cup sprint at its centre, is the highlight of the summer season.

On the Rowley Mile, a series of Flat racing's most important prizes takes place, including the 2000 Guineas and the 1000 Guineas, the first Classics of the year, over a mile (1,600m), in May. The 2000 Guineas for colts and fillies was inaugurated in 1809 when the two thousand guineas prize was won by Wizard. Since then some of the sport's great names have been successful, including Gladiateur (1863), Ormonde (1886), Sceptre (1902), Tudor Minstrel (1947), Nijinsky (1970), Brigadier Gerard (1971), Dancing Brave (1986), Nashwan (1989), Sea The Stars (2009) and Frankel (2011).

Five years after the 2000 Guineas was inaugurated, Charlotte won the first staging of the fillies-only 1000 Guineas – with an eponymous prize; Formosa (1868) and Sceptre (1902) are the only fillies to have won both Guineas races, though the former dead-heated against the colts. Other notable winners include Pretty Polly (1904), Sun Chariot (1942) and Oh So Sharp (1985).

The seven-furlong (1,400m), Group One Dewhurst Stakes, staged since 1875, is the principal two-year-old race of the year, and is part of 'Future Champions Day', now the autumn's feature after 'Champions Day' was transferred away to Ascot. An illustration perhaps that although Newmarket remains 'Headquarters', its one-time position as Britain's premier racecourse is not as undisputed as it used to be.

York

United Kingdom

LOCATION: TWO MILES (3.2KM) SOUTHWEST OF YORK CITY CENTRE

THE TRACK: LEVEL, LEFT-HANDED, TRIANGULAR WITH CHUTES, TURF, JUST UNDER TWO MILES (3,200M) ROUND

PRINCIPAL RACES: INTERNATIONAL STAKES, YORKSHIRE OAKS, NUNTHORPE STAKES, ALL IN AUGUST

OPENED: 1731

FAMOUS MOMENTS: 100,000 WATCH MATCH-RACE BETWEEN VOLTIGEUR AND THE FLYING DUTCHMAN, 1851

There are no three-legged mares to be found at York races these days, but for hundreds of years until the early nineteenth century, the gallows – nicknamed the 'three-legged mare' – at the Knavesmire racecourse greeted travellers into York. Indeed, public executions, most famously that of the highwayman Dick Turpin in 1739 for horse stealing, were a grizzly side-attraction for racegoers as fixtures regularly occurred at the same time as the assizes.

More than one theory abounds as to why the large, low-lying area of land close to the River Ouse is known as the Knavesmire, but most satisfying is the connection to knaves like Turpin receiving justice, and the sometimes boggy ground conditions.

Racing in York dates back to Roman times, taking place in a number of locations in and around the ancient city until settling at the Knavesmire, probably in 1731. What is believed to have

been the first viewing stand on a British racecourse, designed by the accomplished Yorkshire architect John Carr, was opened in the 1750s; parts remain today, making it the oldest stand in use in world sport. Work has continued regularly since, and in the Melrose, Knavesmire and Ebor Stands, York has developed some of the most popular facilities in British racing, ensuring eight Racecourse of the Year awards.

These days a crowd of 42,500 is a sell-out, but in 1851 it is said that 100,000 arrived to see two arch-rivals, Voltigeur and The Flying Dutchman, take on each other in a match-race. Both Epsom Derby and St Leger winners, the five-year-old The Flying Dutchman gained revenge for a previous defeat by his younger opponent, but Voltigeur is better remembered, with the Great Voltigeur Stakes taking place at the Ebor Festival in August.

Other horses to be honoured with races are the Yorkshire-trained Classic-race winners Dante and Musidora – whose races are staged at the Dante Festival meeting in May – and Gimcrack, 'the little grey horse' which won twenty-seven out of his thirty-six races in the mid-eighteenth century. The Gimcrack Stakes, also

in August, is a race for two-year-olds, after which the winning owner makes a speech at the annual dinner of the Gimcrack Club (formed in 1767) in December, although he or she is no longer required to provide 'six dozen bottles of champagne'.

York has earned a reputation for mixing the old with the new, and while traditions like the Gimcrack Dinner continue, significant new races have been introduced. In August 1972, a small but high-quality field contested the first Benson and Hedges Gold Cup – now the International Stakes – for which the unbeaten Brigadier Gerard started as odds-on favourite. However, that year's Derby winner Roberto, ridden from the front by the US-based, Panamanian-born jockey Braulio Baeza, inflicted the sole defeat Brigadier Gerard suffered in eighteen races. The encounter – the course record time was broken by first and second – ensured the race quickly gained a reputation as a significant high-summer prize, and it has since been won by a series of high-quality performers.

In 2008 the race was staged at Newmarket because flooding caused the cancellation of the whole Ebor Festival; they do not call it the Knavesmire for nothing.

North America

Garrison Savannah

Barbados

LOCATION: TWO MILES (3.2KM) SOUTHEAST OF BRIDGETOWN
THE TRACK: RIGHT-HANDED, OVAL, TURF; THREE-QUARTERS OF A MILE (1,200M) ROUND, WITH A SHARP FINAL BEND; THREE SEASONS: SPRING (JANUARY–APRIL), SUMMER (MAY–SEPTEMBER) AND WINTER (NOVEMBER–DECEMBER)

PRINCIPAL RACES: BARBADOS GOLD CUP, MARCH
OPENED: 1845

Barbados is probably better known for cricket than for horseracing, but Garrison Savannah racecourse outside Bridgetown has some twenty-five years on the island's Kensington Oval cricket ground. Both have origins rooted in colonialism, and British soldiers were racing their horses against those of wealthy locals on the parade ground outside their barracks well before the first properly organised fixture in 1845.

The Barbados Turf Club – formed in 1905 – usually stages fixtures on alternate Saturdays. Many days have their own theme – the Betting Booth Staff Appreciation Raceday in May catches the eye as a nice gesture – but the highlight of the year takes place in March: the Barbados Gold Cup, the premier horseracing event in the Caribbean. Upwards of 30,000 racegoers squeeze into the track for what has become a national event, many taking advantage of the opportunity Garrison Savannah provides to be right on top of the action by crowding deep around the rails, while others watch from the shade of the many trees lining the track.

The Barbados Gold Cup is staged over one and a half circuits of the tight turf track. It is open to international runners, and has seen contenders from America and Canada in the line-up, but horses bred in the West Indies receive a seven-pound weight allowance. Since Trinidad entrant Bold Lewis won the inaugural running in 1982, winners have included Sandford Prince (three times) and Chou Chou Royale; between them, the pair gave legendary jockey-turned-trainer Scobie Breasley four successes in the race. The 1997 winner Incitatus later raced in Canada, where success at Grade Two level at Woodbine in Toronto made him the first Barbados-bred horse to win a Graded race in North America.

The Barbadian Triple Crown takes place between April and August and includes the Guineas over just less than a mile (1,570m), the Midsummer Creole Classic over a mile and an eighth (1,800m) and the Barbados Derby over one and a quarter miles (2,000m).

Away from Garrison Savannah, two mornings a week, horses trained at the track are permitted to a 'soak' in the sea at a nearby beach. Quite a cool sight.

Hastings Park
Canada

LOCATION: FOUR MILES (6.4KM) EAST OF CENTRAL VANCOUVER

THE TRACK: LEFT-HANDED, OVAL, DIRT OF JUST OVER FIVE FURLONGS (1,069M); MEETINGS HELD FROM APRIL TO OCTOBER, USUALLY ON SATURDAYS OR SUNDAYS

PRINCIPAL RACES: BRITISH COLUMBIA DERBY, SEPTEMBER

OPENED: 1989

FAMOUS MOMENTS: MULTIPLE TRACK CHAMPION CHRIS LOSETH EQUALS THE THEN NORTH AMERICAN RECORD FOR WINNERS IN A DAY WHEN RIDING EIGHT AT A FIXTURE IN APRIL 1984

There is a view from the front of Vancouver's venerable racecourse that even season ticket holders would never tire of. Just beyond the back straight of the track is the Burrard Inlet, flowing into the Pacific, and beyond that the vast vista of the North Shore mountains.

Built on land that used to be part of New Brighton, a popular nineteenth century holiday hotspot, Hastings used to be known as East Park before modernisation. A 5,000-seater tiered grandstand was opened in 1965.

It was once a playground of the famous, including actors Bob Hope and John Wayne, but Canadian racing's stock has fallen since those days, and Hastings even faced closure around 2011 with poor returns from a huge investment in slot machines. One man who helped to raise the venue's profile was Mario Gutierrez, a Mexican jockey who had moved to the city and ended up winning the 2012 Kentucky Derby and Preakness Stakes on I'll Have Another.

Aside from the horses, the Wiener Dog Racing Weekend each July has become a tradition, with the Dachshunds competing against each other on the track.

Woodbine
Canada

LOCATION: FOURTEEN MILES (22.5KM) NORTHWEST OF CENTRAL TORONTO

THE TRACK: LEFT-HANDED, OVAL WITH CHUTES; TURF TRACK OF ONE AND A HALF MILES (2,400M) WITH 479-YARD (438M) HOME STRAIGHT; DIRT TRACK OF ONE MILE (1,610M) WITH 328-YARD (300M) HOME STRAIGHT; RACING FROM APRIL TO DECEMBER

PRINCIPAL RACES: E. P. TAYLOR STAKES, OCTOBER; CANADIAN INTERNATIONAL, OCTOBER

OPENED: 1956

No person has been more significant for Woodbine racecourse – or indeed for horseracing in Canada – than Edward Plunket 'E. P.' Taylor. A highly successful owner and breeder, he was chief steward of the Jockey Club of Canada and president of the Ontario Jockey Club. He was also clearly quite some guy: during the Second World War, he ran supply routes from North America for Winston Churchill. Taylor won Woodbine's historic Queen's Plate fifteen times, notably with the great Northern Dancer, whom he also bred.

After victory in the 1964 Queen's Plate, Northern Dancer, the first Canadian-bred horse to win the Kentucky Derby, was retired to stud where he became probably the most influential stallion ever. The Taylor family's prolific breeding operation based at Windfields Farm no longer exists, but its legacy certainly does. Woodbine's Grade One Northern Dancer Turf Stakes takes place in September over a full circuit of the one-and-a-half-mile (2,400m) E. P. Taylor turf course. And it could not be more appropriate that the Grade One E. P. Taylor Stakes, staged over one and a quarter miles (2,000m) in October – as well as the mile-and-a-half (2,400m) long Canadian International, in the same month – have gained world-class reputations, just as Taylor had envisaged.

Racing began at a 'first' Woodbine racecourse in 1874; the 'new' Woodbine opened its doors, close to Toronto Pearson Airport, in 1956, although the original track continued until 1993, latterly as Greenwood. Thoroughbred Flat racing has been staged alongside harness racing, however, the harness racing is on the move to nearby Mohawk Racetrack, making way for a another turf course.

Woodbine is home to Canadian Horse Racing's Hall of Fame, and also echoes to the sound of thousands of slot machines. There are facilities for the training of up to 2,175 horses.

The Queen's Plate, originally donated by Queen Victoria and first staged in 1860, is the first part of the Triple Crown, open to Canadian-bred horses; it is staged over a mile and a quarter (2,000m) in June on an artificial surface. Leg two, in July, is on the dirt surface at Fort Erie, while the runners return to Woodbine for the one and a half miles (2,400m) of the Breeders' Stakes in August.

It is perhaps no great surprise that the first two Triple Crown winners were owned and bred by E. P. Taylor.

Martinique

Martinique

LOCATION: CLOSE TO THE INTERNATIONAL AIRPORT AT LE LAMENTIN, SIX MILES (9.7KM) EAST OF FORT-DE-FRANCE

THE TRACK: LEFT-HANDED CIRCUIT OF A MILE AND ONE FURLONG (1,800M), GRASS WITH TROTTING TRACK INSIDE; FIXTURES ARE SPREAD THROUGHOUT THE YEAR

FAMOUS MOMENTS: THE RACECOURSE BEING RENAMED IN 2016 AFTER MAURICE BRUERE-DAWSON, THE MODERN FATHER OF RACING IN MARTINIQUE

They amuse themselves in unusual ways in Martinique, the small rocky Caribbean island with a population of around 385,000. Along with the usually frowned-upon activities of cock-fighting and bouts between snakes and mongooses, racing is a national sport.

There is just the one small track, in the lower-lying and more industrial part of the French overseas department, backing onto the airport. While the track itself is basic, this should not detract from its charms. It is lively, colourful and with beautiful tree-covered paddocks and grounds, full of bougainvillea and bird of paradise flowers. A small grandstand, which can hold 1,000 people, was part of a renovation in 2002 which enhanced the course's tropical style.

The racing is not of a high standard, usually with small fields of moderate horses, but it falls under the auspices of the French authorities. Not only has the much-decorated rider Yves Saint-Martin visited, he even has a race named after him.

Leading jockey Didier Gengoul moved to Britain in 2017. Despite being 46 years of age and 23-times champion at home, there was some confusion, as only 76 of his winners had come under France Galop's jurisdiction, meaning that he could still be classed as an apprentice overseas.

Mexico City

Mexico

LOCATION: FOUR MILES (6.4KM) WEST OF THE CENTRE OF MEXICO CITY, NEAR THE DESIRABLE NEIGHBOURHOOD OF LOMAS DE CHAPULTEPEC
THE TRACK: LEFT-HANDED, OVAL, DIRT TRACK OF SEVEN FURLONGS (1,400M); MEETINGS FRIDAY–SUNDAY ELEVEN MONTHS OF THE YEAR
PRINCIPAL RACES: DERBY MEXICANO, JULY; HANDICAP DE LAS AMERICAS, MAY
OPENED: 1943

FAMOUS MOMENTS: US TRIPLE CROWN-WINNING JOCKEY VICTOR ESPINOZA RIDES HIS FIRST-EVER WINNER AT THE TRACK IN JUNE 1992; HE HAD ONCE PAID FOR HIS TUITION BY DRIVING BUSES

Mexico's most famous racecourse used to be Agua Caliente in Tijuana, which drew the phenomenal Phar Lap from Australia in 1932, but it is now defunct. It is a pity that the last remaining arena for thoroughbred racing is not a big part of the psyche of the capital's population, as it is pretty spectacular.

The track was financed by the Italian industrialist Bruno Pagliai, who was thwarted in his attempt to build a track in Las Vegas but found a friendlier ear in the horse-loving President Camacho. Allocated a fifty-acre slice of military land, the place boomed for the next couple of decades, and while many fewer attend nowadays because of a perception perhaps that horseracing is elitist, the racecourse has benefitted from excellent recent investment.

Not only does it have a large, multi-tiered paddock and immaculately landscaped terrain, it has a host of restaurants and hi-tech facilities for the 1,300 horses trained on site. They are not all thoroughbreds, with so-called 'bullet' sprint races staged for specialist 'quarter' horses regularly included on the cards.

Panama City

Panama

LOCATION: FIVE MILES (8KM) EAST OF CENTRAL PANAMA CITY

THE TRACK: LEFT-HANDED, OVAL OF ONE MILE (1,600M), DIRT, WITH TRAINING TRACK INSIDE; MEETINGS THROUGH THE YEAR ON THURSDAY EVENINGS, SATURDAYS AND SUNDAYS

PRINCIPAL RACES: GRAN CLÁSICO PRESIDENTE DE LA REPÚBLICA, MAY/JUNE

OPENED: 1956

Panama's only racecourse is named the Hipódromo Presidente Remón after the country's leader General José Antonio Remón Cantera, a significant racing fan who was behind the project to build this new track. But while attending a meeting at the dilapidated Juan Franco racecourse in 1955, he was ambushed and assassinated.

His 'baby' opened a year later close to stadiums named after five of Panama's greatest sportspeople: boxer Roberto Durán, swimmer Eileen Coparropa, long-jumper Irving Saladino and footballers Luis Ernesto Tapia and Rommel Fernández.

The racecourse itself has some distinguished alumni, as this small border country excels at producing jockeys. Braulio Baeza rode Roberto to inflict the only defeat on the great colt Brigadier Gerard in the first Benson & Hedges Gold Cup at York in 1972; while US Hall of Famers Laffit Pincay Jr and Alex Solis also cut their teeth here.

Crowds are not large, aside from the day of the Gran Clásico Presidente de la República, but the course's fortunes have improved since it moved out of state-run hands in 1997.

Canóvanas

Puerto Rico

LOCATION: TWENTY MILES (32.2KM) EAST OF THE CAPITAL SAN JUAN

THE TRACK: LEFT-HANDED, DIRT CIRCUIT, ONE MILE (1,600M); FIXTURES THROUGHOUT THE YEAR SATURDAY—MONDAY, WEDNESDAY AND FRIDAY

PRINCIPAL RACES: CLÁSICO LUIS MUÑOZ RIVERA MEMORIAL, JULY; CLÁSICO CAMARERO

OPENED: 1976

FAMOUS MOMENTS: DONA CHEPA'S LAST PLACE IN A RACE IN 2007 BEING HER 125TH DEFEAT IN A ROW, ESTABLISHING WHAT IS BELIEVED TO BE THE LONGEST LOSING RECORD IN RACING HISTORY

Originally known as El Nuevo Comandante, this has been Puerto Rico's only racecourse since 1972. When facing bankruptcy and sold to local owners in 2007, its name was changed to Hipódromo Camarero. A small but talented horse in the 1950s, Camarero never raced outside Puerto Rico but established a world-record unbeaten streak of fifty-six in a row.

Camarero is a modern arena, with an indoor restaurant and bar and an attractive view over large lakes in the middle. There is barely a day when the place is not open, with eight race meetings five times a week, and simulcast action to gamble on during blank afternoons.

It has seen some fine Puerto Rican-bred horses, such as 1989's champion two-year-old Mister Frisky who went on to take third place in US racing's Preakness Stakes despite being found to have an abscess in his oesophagus. And some brilliant native jockeys include world-leading money-earner John Velazquez and brothers Irad and Jose Ortiz, all of whom trained at the apprentice school.

Disaster struck in September 2017 when Hurricane Maria left barns damaged, some horses fatally injured and others without hay or clean water; nevertheless, the course was able to stage a fixture the following month.

Santa Rosa Park

Trinidad & Tobago

LOCATION: IN THE TOWN OF ARIMA, IN THE MIDDLE OF THE ISLAND OF TRINIDAD

THE TRACK: LEFT-HANDED, OVAL, DIRT TRACK OF JUST OVER A MILE (1,700M) WITH GRASS TRACK ON INSIDE; THREE OR FOUR MEETINGS PER MONTH, USUALLY ON SATURDAYS, THROUGHOUT THE YEAR

PRINCIPAL RACES: ROYAL OAK DERBY, SEPTEMBER

OPENED: 1994

FAMOUS MOMENTS: BRUCEONTHELOOSE, THREE-TIME HORSE OF THE YEAR AND CHAMPION IN EVERYTHING FROM SPRINTS TO STAYING RACES, BEING BURIED ON THE INFIELD FOLLOWING HIS DEATH IN 2013

It is somewhat of a shame that Trinidad & Tobago no longer has the variety of racecourses of old: there has been racing in different corners of the islands for more than two centuries, and a grand project near Port of Spain costing millions was abandoned after a year's construction in 1981 because of allegations of corruption and a desire for houses instead.

Happily, Santa Rosa Park, which cost a far more conservative amount – with a decent grandstand, stabling for around 600 horses and a training facility – stepped into its place. There is controlled gambling and a vibrant and competitive local scene, with plenty of long-established prizes and a Trinidad Triple Crown, played out in front of a glorious backdrop of green hilly countryside.

Top jockey Frankie Dettori was the star attraction in late 2014 when he led a star-studded international team including Kieren Fallon and Jamie Spencer in a jockeys' challenge. Although they lost to the local side overall, Dettori still won the feature Caribbean Champion Stakes in a track record time on the local hero Bigman In Town, an appropriate name indeed.

Arlington

United States of America

LOCATION: ARLINGTON HEIGHTS, A SUBURB OF CHICAGO 30 MILES (48.3KM) NORTHWEST OF THE CENTRE

THE TRACK: LEFT-HANDED, ALL-WEATHER OVAL OF A MILE AND ONE FURLONG (1,800M), TURF COURSE WITH BANKED CORNERS INSIDE; MEETINGS FROM MAY TO SEPTEMBER

PRINCIPAL RACES: ARLINGTON MILLION, BEVERLY D. STAKES, BOTH IN AUGUST

OPENED: 1927

FAMOUS MOMENTS: HOSTING THE WORLD'S FIRST MILLION-DOLLAR TURF RACE, THE ARLINGTON MILLION, IN 1981, WON BY JOHN HENRY AND JOCKEY BILL SHOEMAKER, WHO ARE IMMORTALISED BY A STATUE OVERLOOKING THE PADDOCK

Arlington is part of the huge Chicago conurbation and even has its own station on a line leading to the city, although spectators might not be able to tell that from the enormous grandstand capable of holding 50,000. Looking outwards, the view is of a beautiful parkland course surrounded by oaks and willows, with immaculate hedges and a lake. All around, from the intimate paddock to the traditional-looking buildings, there is that rare sense that all is right with the world.

Arlington has led the way with innovation, installing the first

electronic totalisator board in 1933 and bringing in the first public-address system. Through ambitious marketing it also arranged a much-talked-about match race in 1955 in which Nashua, winner of the Preakness Stakes and Belmont Stakes, got revenge on Swaps for defeat by that horse in the Kentucky Derby.

There have been ups and downs along the way: there was a corruption case in the early 1970s when Otto Kerner, a former governor of Illinois, was convicted of bribery in buying discounted shares in the track in exchange for favourable race dates. Later, Arlington was to land a major coup when general manager Bill Thayer persuaded Penny Chenery, owner of the great Secretariat, to bring the horse to Arlington for an invitational race just a month after he became the first Triple Crown hero in a quarter of a century. Racing for $125,000 against just three rivals, it was to prove a lap of honour for Secretariat in front of a crowd numbering more than 41,000.

Then in 1985 disaster struck when a small fire became an inferno and completely destroyed the grandstand. Remarkably, less than a month later, British gelding Teleprompter won in front of 35,000-plus spectators housed in temporary stands and tents. As a result, Arlington became the first course to receive a coveted Eclipse Award for staging the 'Miracle Million'. The feature race made a brief move to Canada while the splendid new infrastructure was built. At the turn of the twenty-first century there was a break in racing for two years when the racecourse closed temporarily.

The Arlington Million has had some memorable winners, including the Luca Cumani-trained Tolomeo which became the first British-trained horse to land a major American race for over a decade in 1983, while Powerscourt (2005) and Cape Blanco (2011) won for the all-conquering Irish champion trainer Aidan O'Brien.

Belmont Park

United States of America

LOCATION: LONG ISLAND, NEW YORK STATE

THE TRACK: LEFT-HANDED, OVAL, DIRT TRACK OF ONE AND A HALF MILES (2,400M) WITH CHUTE AND 365-YARD (334M) HOME STRAIGHT, TWO INNER TURF TRACKS; RACING APRIL–JULY, SEPTEMBER–OCTOBER

PRINCIPAL RACES: BELMONT STAKES, JUNE

OPENED: 1905

FAMOUS MOMENTS: SECRETARIAT'S WIDE-MARGIN SUCCESS IN THE BELMONT STAKES TO WIN THE 1973 TRIPLE CROWN

Belmont Park is known as 'the Championship Track', as probably all of US racing's champions have competed there. The leafy, tree-lined course is the largest in North America.

Following on from the Kentucky Derby at Churchill Downs and the Preakness Stakes at Pimlico, the Belmont Stakes – the so-called 'Test of the Champion' – is the third and final leg of American racing's Triple Crown. All three races take place on dirt surfaces within a frantic six-week period, with the race on Belmont's 'Big Sandy' track the most examining. The 2004 staging attracted a crowd of 120,000.

Completing the iconic treble is rare – famously the Belmont caller declared excitedly that 'the thirty-seven-year wait is over' when American Pharoah became the twelfth horse to achieve it, in 2015. Number thirteen came just three years later when, remarkably, Justify completed the hat-trick less than four months after making his racecourse debut. The 1970s had proved a golden decade when three horses – Secretariat (1973), Seattle Slew (1977) and Affirmed (1978) – all made their way into the Triple Crown history books, Secretariat perhaps most memorably. By winning the Belmont by thirty-one lengths in a world-record time, Secretariat surpassed the breathtaking twenty-length success of the legendary Man o' War half a century earlier.

The Belmont Stakes was inaugurated in 1867, and so-named after the family that played a significant role in the early days of organised horseracing in New York. The race was staged at Jerome Park and Morris Park tracks before relocating to Long Island when Belmont Park was opened in 1905; the design and layout were based on European courses. Having established itself, Belmont closed for two years in 1911 when New York State law prohibited gambling. Up and running again in 1913, officials set about building the wide-ranging racing programme in which some of the greats of American racing have taken part.

The Breeders' Cup fixture has been staged at Belmont four times and, in 2001, it was the first major sports event in New York after 9/11.

Facilities, for which capacity was finally capped at 90,000 in 2015, underwent a major upgrade in the 1960s, when the track was closed from 1963 to 1968. However, there is regular talk about further development work, particularly to the vast grandstand which, while state-of-the-art when built, feels a little cold and grey in the twenty-first century and also casts a big shadow over the track; infamously, the brilliant British-trained Dayjur jumped a shadow when looking sure of victory and losing the initiative in the 1990 Breeders' Cup Sprint.

Whatever happens inside the course, plans immediately around are extensive, with New York Racing Association's Christopher Kay saying they would attract new customers to the area to the extent that 'horseracing is going to be cool again'.

Churchill Downs

United States of America

LOCATION: LOUISVILLE, KENTUCKY, FOUR AND A HALF MILES (7.25KM) FROM THE CITY CENTRE

THE TRACK: LEFT-HANDED, OVAL; ONE-MILE (1,600M) DIRT TRACK (WITH CHUTE), SEVEN-FURLONG (1,400M) TURF TRACK ON INSIDE; 412-YARD (377M) HOME STRAIGHT; SEASONS IN SPRING, SEPTEMBER AND LATE OCTOBER/NOVEMBER

PRINCIPAL RACES: KENTUCKY DERBY, MAY

OPENED: 1875

Since 1895, the Twin Spires on top of the main grandstand at Churchill Downs racecourse have been a reassuring constant in an ever-developing world. Staring out over the celebrated acres below, they have gained iconic status in horseracing across the globe, and have become symbols of America's most famous race, the Kentucky Derby. Predating the Spires by two decades, the Derby – which forms the first leg of the Triple Crown – has experienced the longest uninterrupted run of any other sporting event in US history.

It was in 1875 that Colonel Meriwether Lewis Clark started what was then the Louisville Jockey Club racetrack on land leased from his uncles Henry and John Churchill (hence the later name change). The Derby, the Kentucky Oaks and the Clark Handicap – races modelled on the British Classics – took place on the opening day.

This was a time when memories of the American Civil War, and the abolition of slavery that followed, remained fresh in people's minds. And the fact that Ansel Williamson, trainer of the first Derby winner Aristides, and the successful jockey, nineteen-year-old Oliver Lewis, were both African-Americans from a background of slavery makes the race a not insignificant event in the history of civil rights in the US. The result was held up as evidence of what could be achieved by the black community.

Ten thousand people saw that first Derby; in 2015, a record 170,000 witnessed the race dubbed the 'Run for the Roses' – the winner receives a garland of roses – or 'the most exciting two minutes in sports'. Around eighty thousand spectators usually pack into the twenty-six acres of the infield, a hugely popular attraction famous for its rowdy atmosphere. The drink of choice amongst racegoers is the Mint Julep, a cocktail of bourbon, sprigs of mint and syrup with crushed ice, often served in souvenir glasses.

Since Aristides, an array of US champions has followed him. None has been greater than Secretariat, who set the long-standing record over the mile-and-a-quarter distance (2,000m) – 1 minute, 59.4 seconds – on his way to the 1973 Triple Crown. Analysis of the times for each quarter mile show that this remarkable horse went faster as the race progressed, his exertions apparently not affecting him at all.

While the victory of Secretariat may be amongst the most famous, perhaps the most infamous occurred in 1933, when Brokers Tip and jockey Don Meade narrowly beat Herb Fisher's mount, Head Play, in what became known as the 'Fighting Finish'. Near the end of the race, Fisher leaned across and pulled at Meade's saddle, while for his part Meade grabbed his rival's shoulder; the bad-tempered encounter continued in the changing room afterwards.

The Derby is the centrepiece of the Spring meet at Churchill Downs, and the Breeders' Cup is a regular visitor. With these two events, a place in civil rights history, fisticuffs in the jockeys' room, the Mint Julep and, of course, the Twin Spires, Churchill Downs really does have a bit of everything.

Del Mar

United States of America

LOCATION: DEL MAR FAIRGROUNDS, ON THE CALIFORNIAN COAST TWENTY MILES (32.2KM) FROM SAN DIEGO – 'WHERE THE TURF MEETS THE SURF'

THE TRACK: LEFT-HANDED, OVAL, ONE MILE (1,600M), FLAT RACING ON DIRT AND TURF; JULY–SEPTEMBER AND NOVEMBER

PRINCIPAL RACES: BING CROSBY STAKES, JULY; PACIFIC CLASSIC STAKES, AUGUST

OPENED: 1937

FAMOUS MOMENTS: SEABISCUIT VERSUS LIGAROTI IN 1938; THE 2017 BREEDERS' CUP

Del Mar holds many reminders of the golden age of Hollywood, when the seaside resort of choice for A-listers was the Del Mar Racetrack. Elegant and relaxed in the southern Californian sunshine, it glories in the slogan 'Nobody's in a hurry except the horses'.

That theme goes back to the very start, in the 1930s, when the singer Bing Crosby resolved to open a racecourse and brought together other big names from the entertainment world to help. Actors including Joe E. Brown, Gary Cooper, Oliver Hardy and Pat O'Brien agreed to join Crosby, along with Jimmy Durante. For business acumen, Charles S. Howard, the owner of the prolific champion racehorse Seabiscuit, was also part of the consortium. When they opened for the first fixture in July 1937, Crosby was one of those manning the turnstiles.

The connection with Howard proved lucrative a year later when Seabiscuit, 1938's Horse of the Year, was brought to Del Mar for a $25,000 winner-takes-all match race against Crosby's and Lindsay Howard's horse Ligaroti. Seabiscuit, the subject of the 2003 Hollywood movie, was a major draw, and the stands were packed. After a tense duel, Seabiscuit won by a nose; the showdown was front-page news across America.

The standing of Del Mar grew markedly. Crosby sold his share in the racecourse in 1946, but to this day, the song he penned about the racetrack is played on every race-day:

Where the turf meets the surf
Down at old Del Mar
Take a plane
Take a train
Take a car.
There's a smile on every face
And a winner in each race
Where the turf meets the surf
At Del Mar.

The staging of the Bing Crosby Handicap in July and the Bing Crosby Meet during November are also regular reminders of how things first started.

In 1956, it was at Del Mar that John Longden broke jockey legend Sir Gordon Richards' record of 4,870 winners. Fourteen years later, also at Del Mar, Bill Shoemaker passed Longden's record.

The 1990s proved a busy decade for Del Mar with major renovations and the introduction in 1991 of the richest race of the year, the Grade One Pacific Classic, a 'win and you're in' qualifier for the Breeders' Cup Classic that has become one of America's most prestigious races of its type.

In 2017, Del Mar became the twelfth racecourse in North America to stage the Breeders' Cup fixture, the 'World Championships' of horseracing, attracting runners from around the globe. How Bing Crosby would have crooned.

Gulfstream Park

United States of America

LOCATION: HALLANDALE BEACH, BETWEEN FORT LAUDERDALE AND MIAMI

THE TRACK: LEFT-HANDED, OVAL, DIRT TRACK OF ONE AND AN EIGHTH MILES (1,800M) WITH BACKSTRETCH CHUTE, ONE MILE (1,600M) TURF ON INSIDE, 328-YARD (300M) HOME STRAIGHT

PRINCIPAL RACES: PEGASUS WORLD CUP, SUNSHINE MILLIONS, BOTH JANUARY

OPENED: 1939

FAMOUS MOMENTS: JOCKEY BILL SHOEMAKER WON HIS FINAL RACE HERE IN 1990

Under the guidance of racecourse entrepreneur Frank Stronach and The Stronach Group, Gulfstream Park, located eighteen miles (29km) up the Florida coast from Miami, has bloomed in the glow of the Sunshine State. With a year-round fixture list, the racing, staged alongside a casino, shopping mall and office complex following a $170 million refurbishment, accounts for an ever-growing proportion of wagers staked across the United States. And while high-profile events like the Breeders' Cup – staged at Gulfstream three times, in 1989, 1992 and 1999 – may be a thing of the past, it is now home to the richest horse race on the globe: the Pegasus World Cup.

Inaugurated in 2017 for $12 million, with the promise of an immediate rise to $16 million for 2018, the race replaces the Donn Handicap and is staged on dirt over one and an eighth miles (1,800m). The twelve berths in the gate cost $1 million each and, under the conditions of the race, the purchaser can sell their place in the line-up if they do not have a horse for it.

A vast bronze of Pegasus, the winged horse of legend, battling with a dragon stands in its own park at the north entrance; it is one of the tallest statues in the United States.

Other major events at Gulfstream Park include the Sunshine Millions Series in January, where the races are shared with The Stronach Group's track at Santa Anita, California, and are open only to horses bred in Florida and California. The Florida Derby, held in March, is an important part of the build-up to the US Triple Crown, particularly the Kentucky Derby. Amongst the horses to have won both are Northern Dancer, Unbridled, Thunder Gulch and Big Brown.

In 1964, Northern Dancer, later one of the great stallions and breeding influences of all time, was ridden to victory by record-breaking jockey Bill Shoemaker. 'The Shoe' partnered the last of his 8,833 winners, Beau Genius, at Gulfstream in January 1990 before retiring the following month.

Keeneland

United States of America

LOCATION: WEST OF LEXINGTON, KENTUCKY

THE TRACK: LEFT-HANDED, OVAL, ONE-AND-ONE-SIXTEENTH-MILE (1,710M) DIRT COURSE WITH CHUTES, JUST UNDER ONE-MILE (1,450M) TURF, HOME STRAIGHT OF 390 YARDS (357M); RACING FESTIVALS IN APRIL AND OCTOBER

PRINCIPAL RACES: BLUE GRASS STAKES, APRIL

OPENED: 1936

The traditional and conservative Keeneland Racetrack holds a special place in the horse-mad state of Kentucky. Built on 147 acres of farmland sold by Jack Keene, from whom the racecourse gets its name, it has become a biannual pilgrimage for passionate American racing fans.

Opened in 1935, with racing beginning a year later, it was primarily a sales arena that went on to become the world's largest thoroughbred auction house. Three major sales events are conducted throughout the year. Prominent equine stars like Zenyatta, Alysheba and Curlin all went under the hammer here, and in 2016 Keeneland Sales provided all three winners of the Triple Crown races: Nyquist (Kentucky Derby), Exaggerator (Preakness) and Creator (Belmont).

In the spring festival, the races form key Kentucky Derby preparation races, including the Blue Grass Stakes, won in 1964 by the great Northern Dancer, who went on to win the Kentucky Derby and ultimately take the breeding world by storm. In the autumn festival, Keeneland's races serve as prep races for the Breeders' Cup championships.

The course's founders were adamant that Keeneland would remain a traditional sporting venue, and it has been viewed as a track reluctant to change. As recently as 1997, it became the last American track to broadcast commentary over the public-address system, and its largely unchanged landscape has given it a very retro feel. As a result, the track was used for both of the famous racing films *Seabiscuit* and *Secretariat*. It became a National Historic Landmark in 1986.

Probably, Keeneland's greatest moment came in its selection to hold the 2015 Breeders' Cup, in what turned out to be a stellar year for American racing. Breaking a thirty-seven-year drought, American Pharoah had won the Triple Crown in the June, but came to the Breeders' Cup on the back of defeat in the Travers Stakes at Saratoga in the August. However, American Pharoah did not disappoint this time, soaring to a scintillating six-and-a-half lengths' success over older horses and old foes.

It was the first time any horse had completed the unofficial 'Grand Slam' of American horseracing (the Triple Crown and Breeders' Cup Classic). With track attendance records broken despite the small, historic venue, the event earned rave reviews.

Pimlico
United States of America

LOCATION: SEVEN AND A HALF MILES (12KM) NORTHWEST OF THE CENTRE OF BALTIMORE, MARYLAND
THE TRACK: LEFT-HANDED, OVAL; DIRT TRACK OF ONE MILE (1,600M) WITH 384-YARD (351M) HOME STRAIGHT; SEVEN-FURLONG (1,400M) TURF TRACK ON INSIDE

PRINCIPAL RACES: PREAKNESS STAKES, MAY
OPENED: 1870
FAMOUS MOMENTS: CONGRESS CLOSED DOWN FOR A DAY SO MEMBERS COULD ATTEND 'THE GREAT RACE' AT PIMLICO, 1877

Pimlico racetrack in Maryland thrives on its traditions. Home of the Preakness Stakes, the 'middle jewel' in the US Triple Crown, it is the second oldest track in America, after Saratoga. The crowds who pour in every May for the Preakness – 140,000-plus – can sense the history, even if some of them perhaps feel that the facilities could do with a modernising touch. In fact, they can even see history in action. Immediately on confirmation of the winner, the course weather vane is painted in the colours of the successful owner's silks, just as has happened since 1909.

A painter is hoisted on a hydraulic lift to the horse and jockey vane on the replica of the cupola of the original clubhouse – destroyed by fire in 1966 – in the winner's circle. In 1918, when the race was staged in two divisions, one set of colours was up there for six months before being replaced by the other.

The winning horse is shrouded in a blanket of the state's signature Black-Eyed Susan flowers and a three-foot (90cm) tall solid-silver trophy, the Woodlawn Vase – so valuable that it gets a police escort from the Baltimore Museum of Art – is presented before being returned (the owner takes a copy).

The owners of some of American racing's greatest horses have seen their colours displayed on the weather vane: clearly, all winners of the Triple Crown, plus Man o' War (1920), Challedon (1939), Northern Dancer (1964), Spectacular Bid (1979), Sunday Silence (1989), Summer Squall (1990), Curlin (2007) and California Chrome (2014). Gallant Fox, the Triple Crown winner of 1930, is the only horse to have taken the Preakness leg on one of the eleven occasions when it took place before the Kentucky Derby.

Just like the Derby at Epsom, the Preakness originated from an idea put up at a high-society party; guests agreed to race their horses against each other at Pimlico, so-named by seventeenth century British settlers in honour of their pub in London. The aptly named Dinner Party Stakes was staged in 1870, and won by a horse called Preakness whose name was given to the Preakness Stakes when it started three years later. Although relocated to New York State from 1894, the race has been back at Pimlico since 1909, taking place on the third Saturday in May as highlight of the sole meet in May. The month also sees the Black-Eyed Susan Stakes and Pimlico Special, in which Seabiscuit beat War Admiral in a much-anticipated showdown in 1938.

Fixtures are run in conjunction with Pimlico's sister track which is also run by the Maryland Jockey Club, twenty-five miles (40.2km) away at Laurel Park.

Santa Anita Park

United States of America

LOCATION: ARCADIA, SEVENTEEN MILES (27.4KM) NORTHEAST OF CENTRAL LOS ANGELES

THE TRACK: LEFT-HANDED, OVAL; DIRT TRACK OF ONE MILE (1,600M) INSIDE TURF TRACK OF SEVEN FURLONGS (1,400M), SEPARATE DOWNHILL TURF COURSE OF A LITTLE OVER SIX FURLONGS (1,290M), HOME STRAIGHT OF 328 YARDS (300M); WINTER-SPRING SEASON FROM DECEMBER TO JUNE AND AUTUMN SEASON OCTOBER–NOVEMBER

PRINCIPAL RACES: SANTA ANITA HANDICAP, MARCH; SANTA ANITA DERBY, APRIL

OPENED: 1934

FAMOUS MOMENTS: FREQUENT HOME OF THE BREEDERS' CUP

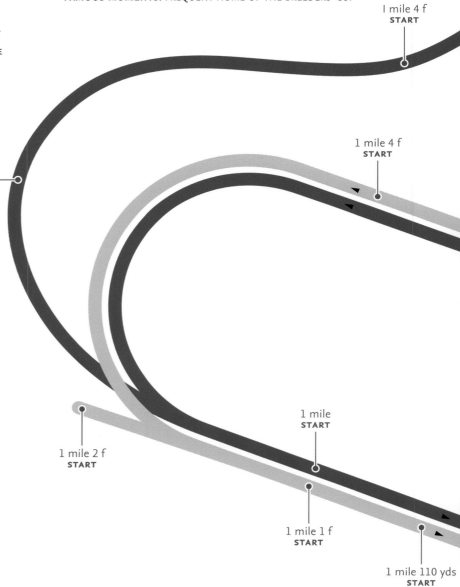

1 mile 4 f
START

1 mile 4 f
START

1 mile 2 f
START

1 mile 2 f
START

1 mile
START

1 mile 1 f
START

1 mile 110 yds
START

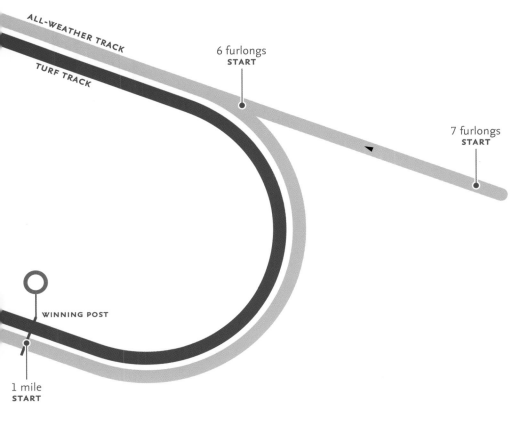

6 furlongs 110 yds
START

ALL-WEATHER TRACK

TURF TRACK

6 furlongs
START

7 furlongs
START

WINNING POST

1 mile
START

Many racecourses around the world claim to be the most picturesque place for horseracing there is, but unlike Santa Anita, they do not have the backdrop of the San Gabriel mountains. However bad a day is being experienced at the races, one glance at the rugged scenery towering over the track, generally framed by blue skies, is enough to lift the spirits. And the stunning vista does not end there: the course is lined with a mass of greenery, including strikingly tall palm trees stretching upwards towards the warm southern Californian sun. This 'Great Race Place' feels like something of an oasis just up the freeway from the centre of Los Angeles, a sensation only added to by the many original 1930s buildings.

Racing in the area was started by a hugely successful businessman and racehorse owner named Elias J. 'Lucky' Baldwin in the early years of the twentieth century, on a site close to the current location. The racecourse closed after Baldwin's death but following changes to the betting laws in the 1930s, two Californian entrepreneurs, dentist Charles H. Strub and film producer Hal Roach, joined forces to establish the Los Angeles Turf Club. Santa Anita opened at Christmas 1934 as the first official racecourse in California, and was soon thriving.

Supported by many of the stars from nearby Hollywood, Strub and his team excelled at marketing and promotions, and on the track they pioneered services including photo finish cameras. Putting up, within months, a mind-bogglingly large purse of $100,000 for the inaugural Santa Anita Handicap – at the time the largest ever prize offered in the United States – certainly helped to make an impact.

To this day, the Grade One race, 'The Big' Cap' – staged over one and a quarter miles (2,000m) for three-year-old horses and older – is one of the most prestigious prizes of its type in North America's racing calendar. 'The Big' Cap' takes a leading role in the multi-Oscar-nominated movie *Seabiscuit*, which was partly filmed at Santa Anita. It tells the story of the rags-to-riches horse who became a people's favourite during the Great

Depression and suffered narrow defeats in the 1937 and 1938 stagings before returning, along with his jockey 'Red' Pollard, from career-threatening injury, to score a runaway victory in front of nearly 70,000 cheering spectators in 1940. It was the horse's swansong – how could he top that? – but his legend lives on in the well-cultivated grounds, not least as his statue, one of several impressive pieces around the enclosures, commands pride of place.

Other high-profile winners of the Santa Anita Handicap, which takes place in March, include John Henry (twice – he gets a statue too) and 1978 Triple Crown champion Affirmed. The Santa Anita Derby and Santa Anita Oaks – both Grade Ones that also date back to 1935 – take place in April, while the Grade One Zenyatta Stakes, replacing the Lady's Secret Stakes, is part of the Autumn Meet in October. Zenyatta won 'her' race three years on the trot when it was still known as the Lady's Secret Stakes, those successes coming during a record-breaking run of nineteen consecutive wins.

The Breeders' Cup, US racing's premier fixture, which takes place at the end of October or beginning of November, moves around North America, but has been staged at Santa Anita most often. International raiders relish the chance of a visit to southern California, even if they are faced with the twin challenges of formidable opposition and quite possibly very different weather conditions to back home. However, the influx of horses for the various Breeders' Cup events is as nothing compared to 1984 when the racecourse was used for most of the equestrian disciplines during the Los Angeles Olympics.

When taking place at Santa Anita, the Breeders' Cup comes at the end of the two-month Autumn Meet. The fixture list swelled when nearby Hollywood Park closed its gates, and around 1,980 horses are trained at the track. The owners have long-term plans to expand the number of race-days, stabling and gambling opportunities, leading to much-needed extra revenue.

One thing that no one will ever change is, of course, those mountains. Thank goodness for that.

Saratoga
United States of America

LOCATION: SARATOGA SPRINGS, UPSTATE NEW YORK

THE TRACK: LEFT-HANDED, ALMOST RECTANGULAR WITH THREE RACETRACKS: MAIN DIRT TRACK OF NINE FURLONGS (1,800M); TURF TRACK OF ONE MILE (1,600M); INNER, TURF JUMP-RACING TRACK OF SEVEN FURLONGS (1,400M); RACING JULY TO SEPTEMBER

PRINCIPAL RACES: THE TRAVERS, AUGUST

OPENED: 1864

FAMOUS MOMENTS: THE GREAT MAN O' WAR'S ONLY DEFEAT HERE BEGAN THE 'CURSE' THAT HAS LED TO SARATOGA'S REPUTATION AS THE 'GRAVEYARD OF CHAMPIONS'

One of the oldest sporting venues in the United States, Saratoga has a history dating back to the 1840s. In 1847, standardbred racing was conducted on land opposite the current thoroughbred track, an area once called Horse Haven, but now known as the Oklahoma Training Track. When casino operator, congressman and gambler John Morrissey organised the first fixture for thoroughbreds, it was conducted on this track, and a year later moved to its current home where a large, ornate grandstand was erected.

The Saratoga meet began originally as just four days, but it has gradually expanded to forty, spread out over six weeks of the late summer. Despite longevity, its future has not always been as bright, including in 1911 and 1912, when the racecourse was shut down over anti-gambling legislation (the Hart-Agnew Law). However, in 1919 and 1920, it became associated with Man o' War, one of US racing's greatest names and later most influential stallions. Bought for $5,000 at the Saratoga yearling sale, he won twenty of his twenty-one races including the Preakness Stakes and the Belmont Stakes – his owner decided against running him in the Kentucky Derby, so he missed out on the chance to complete what was then the new concept of the US Triple Crown.

However, despite five successes, Man o' War's one and only defeat also came at Saratoga. After a poorly organised official start to the Sanford Memorial Stakes of 1919, the horse was slowly into his stride and then boxed in, but ultimately only narrowly failed to concede a considerable amount of weight to regular rival Upset. The name of the winner was obviously fitting, but although it is believed by some to be the source of the phrase 'caused an upset', the expression can be found to have been in use over forty years earlier.

Man o' War was only the first in a line of champions to be dethroned at the New York track, with star names like Gallant Fox, Secretariat, Rachel Alexandra and American Pharoah all suffering surprise defeats. Gallant Fox and American Pharoah were both beaten in the track's principal prize, the Travers Stakes, after which the winner's colours are painted on the Travers Canoe that sits on the infield pond.

In other traditions at this track full of old-world charm, a spring of the waters that made Saratoga a famous resort is available in the picnic area; the runners are walked through the crowds before their races; and exactly seventeen minutes before every race the hand-rung bell is sounded for the jockeys to enter the paddock.

Saratoga also saw the final race call of legendary commentator, Tom Durkin, in 2014.

South America

San Isidro

Argentina

LOCATION: VERY CLOSE TO THE LA PLATA RIVER, FOURTEEN MILES (22.5KM) NORTH OF CENTRAL BUENOS AIRES

THE TRACK: SWEEPING, LEFT-HANDED, OVAL, TURF TRACK OF A MILE AND THREE-QUARTERS (2,783M) WITH SEVERAL CHUTES, INNER AND OUTER DIRT TRACK; RACING TWO OR THREE TIMES A WEEK THROUGHOUT THE YEAR

PRINCIPAL RACES: GRAN PREMIO INTERNACIONAL CARLOS PELLEGRINI, DECEMBER

OPENED: 1935

FAMOUS MOMENTS: BRAZILIAN JORGE RICARDO BECOMES THE FIRST-EVER JOCKEY TO RIDE 10,000 CAREER WINNERS IN JANUARY 2008, GOING ON TO A LONG-STANDING RIVALRY WITH THE PROLIFIC CALIFORNIAN RUSSELL BAZE

There are few grander places to go racing in the world than San Isidro, located in Buenos Aires' most exclusive suburb. The home of Argentine rugby, it is a place of cobbled streets, riverside clubs and the British colonial legacy. Along with the national sports of football and polo, the empire brought horseracing, and the standard in Buenos Aires is the highest in South America.

San Isidro is not as old or ornate as nearby Palermo, but it is certainly as stylish and holds the best of the turf racing with its outstanding galloping grass circuit. It was built by the Jockey Club with no shortage of thought. Surrounded by parkland and tree-lined avenues it has six different stands, several of them art deco in nature.

100,000 people can be accommodated, though that number was exceeded in the 1952 Gran Premio Carlos Pellegrini, by those who flocked in to follow the previous year's hugely popular winner Yatasto, who was defeated by Branding. Large crowds still come to that event, even if numbers are down for the more humdrum days, and some of the facilities are perhaps a little worn.

Breeding mares were imported from Britain in the late nineteenth century, helping to spawn what has become an excellent Argentinian racing product. More than 7,000 foals are produced every year, many from lavish stud farms in the Buenos Aires region, and their sturdy nature has made them popular in North America.

Forli, who was unbeaten in seven domestic starts including the 1966 Carlos Pellegrini, was transferred at huge expense to the great Californian Charlie Whittingham, but despite impressing his trainer, his career was restricted by injury problems. Tatan, a South American champion in the 1950s, was also moved to the breeding paddocks of Kentucky and proved an influential stallion. More recently there has been Candy Ride, who became the top miler in 2002, having won a maiden race at San Isidro; he won the Pacific Classic at Del Mar. And another graduate of the track, Asiatic Boy, went on to claim a series of successes in the UAE for the South African trainer Mike de Kock.

Not maybe quite as impressive, but equally vast, is the adjacent training centre, with five concentric oval gallops of similar dimensions to the track itself. Around 2,000 horses can be stabled alongside a farrier's school and veterinary facilities.

Cidade Jardim

Brazil

LOCATION: ON THE PINHEIRO RIVER, FOUR MILES (6.4KM) WEST OF THE CENTRE OF SÃO PAULO
THE TRACK: LEFT-HANDED, OVAL, TURF OF A MILE AND THREE FURLONGS (2,200M) WITH A SAND TRACK INSIDE; MEETINGS THROUGHOUT THE YEAR, USUALLY ON SATURDAYS AND MONDAYS
PRINCIPAL RACES: GRAN PRÊMIO DEL JOCKEY CLUB

OPENED: 1941
FAMOUS MOMENTS: GLORIA DE CAMPEAO, THE BRAZILIAN-BRED WINNER OF THE 2010 DUBAI WORLD CUP, TAKING THE 2007 GRANDE PRÊMIO PRESIDENTE ANTONIO T. ASSUMPÇÃO NETTO

São Paulo's urban racecourse, in a pleasant area of a city full of stark contrasts in wealth and poverty, would have been a fine thing when it was opened under a directive from the mayor and the Brazilian Jockey Club. With stands designed by French art deco architect Henri Sajous, it had floors of fine marble and places for the elite to entertain. Nowadays, with a backdrop skyscrapers, it could be the South American version of Flemington in Melbourne.

Unfortunately, having plunged into the red by millions, in 2016 a fire sale of artwork – including porcelain, paintings and a bronze horse by sculptor Victor Brecheret – had to take place to repay government debts.

While there is some good racing, Cidade Jardim has been best known lately for producing jockeys, and two in particular. The apprentice academy has a fine reputation, with only twelve applicants making the cut each year from more than 150 applications.

Silvestre de Sousa and João Moreira were a couple of years apart as young hopefuls and have both made waves around the world. The former came from northern Brazil to learn his trade and became champion apprentice in 2000. He left three years later, spending some time in Ireland and then the north of England before earning his chances through tactical ability and hard work, and becoming champion jockey in Britain. It was harder still for Moreira. While De Sousa had limited contact with horses during his childhood, Moreira loved them, but his family in Curitiba was very poor, and he worked as a stable-hand before getting a break at the academy.

Moreira was disqualified after winning his first two races and, on the final day of his apprenticeship, needed two wins to keep his licence and avoid going back home with his tail between his legs. Begging trainers around the premises, he managed to secure enough rides to achieve the feat by a whisker in the last race. He rode over 1,000 winners in six years, mainly at Cidade Jardim, before breaking records galore in Singapore and Hong Kong.

Some 1,500 horses are trained in the premises, which has also been used for concerts by performers including Elton John and Andrea Bocelli.

Gávea

Brazil

LOCATION: IN THE FASHIONABLE SUBURB OF GÁVEA, NINE MILES (14.5KM) SOUTHWEST OF THE CENTRE OF RIO DE JANEIRO
THE TRACK: LEFT-HANDED, OVAL, ONE-AND-A-QUARTER-MILE (2,000M) TURF OUTSIDE DIRT TRACK, THREE-FURLONG (600M) RUN-IN; RACING FROM FRIDAY TO MONDAY, YEAR-ROUND

PRINCIPAL RACES: GRANDE PRÊMIO BRASIL, JUNE
OPENED: 1926

Lying in the shadows of Corcovado Mountain and Rio's iconic statue of Christ the Redeemer, and no distance from Ipanema beach, Brazil's Hipódromo da Gávea has as memorable a location as any racecourse in the world. Constructed on marshland reclaimed from the Rodrigo de Freitas Lagoon during the 1920s, it opened in 1926 and, in common with other South American courses, retains much of the architectural splendour and exquisite gardens created by its original designers.

The Grande Prêmio Brasil, first run in 1933, is the feature event and takes place in June. A Grade One race for three-year-olds and upwards, it is contested over one and a half miles on turf and can be, it is hoped, a stepping stone towards the Breeders' Cup Turf in the autumn.

Gávea's Carioca Triple Crown – consisting of the Grade One trio of the Grande Prêmio Estado do Rio de Janeiro, the Grande Prêmio Francisco Eduardo de Paula Machado and the Grande Prêmio Cruzeiro do Sul – takes place between January and March or April, and has tended to be easier to win than similar titles elsewhere in the world.

Up to 1,500 horses can be stabled and trained at Gávea, and a jockeys' school has nurtured talent that has subsequently been seen out on the track. Gradually, Brazilian horses, renowned for their durability, have been making an impact outside their own country, as have the country's jockey-exports, notably Hong Kong-based João 'Magic Man' Moreira and British champion Silvestre de Sousa.

Moreira gave a revealing insight into race-riding back home when he said, 'The other jockeys will try and say anything to you to try and get you to collapse mentally. They'll swear at you, say anything they can to get at you – talk about your wife, talk about your kids – they might even threaten to fight you and try to hit you with a whip in a race.'

Even in front of Christ the Redeemer.

Santiago

Chile

LOCATION: DOWNTOWN SANTIAGO, IN THE SHADOW OF THE ANDES

THE TRACK: RIGHT-HANDED, OVAL WITH CHUTES, ONE AND A HALF MILES (2,400M) ON TURF AND SAND; YEAR-ROUND

PRINCIPAL RACES: CLÁSICO EL ENSAYO, NOVEMBER

OPENED: 1870

FAMOUS MOMENTS: THE VISITS OF EX-PRESIDENT THEODORE ROOSEVELT IN 1914 AND QUEEN ELIZABETH II IN 1968

Club Hípico, with striking views of the Andes Mountains, is the oldest racecourse in South America. The original wooden stand was burned to the ground in 1892 and replaced with a magnificent towered building. Standing in elegant gardens, it was designed by the renowned Chilean-American architect Josué Smith Solar and opened in 1923. Smith Solar sought to copy the stands at Longchamp in Paris.

One of three principal courses in Chile, Club Hípico prides itself on its glamorous society visitors, including ex-US President Theodore Roosevelt and Queen Elizabeth II, as well as the top-level races it stages. These include the Group One Clásico El Ensayo staged over one and a half miles (2,400 metres) in November. With the Clásico St Leger (a mile and three furlongs or 2,200m) on a dirt surface at Hipódromo Chile, also in Santiago, and El Derby (one and a half miles or 2,400m on turf) at the Valparaiso Sporting Club, on the coast, the El Ensayo is part of Chilean racing's National Triple Crown.

Most revered amongst El Ensayo winners is perhaps Wolf, winner in the 1990–91 season, who was undefeated in ten starts – including in the Triple Crown races – and named Chile's Horse of the Century. Sold to race in the United States, he was not able to reproduce quite the same form on a more competitive platform, though he did win races before being retired to stud.

Club Hípico also stages a Triple Crown of its own, with the Premio Polla de Potrillos for colts and geldings, the Premio Polla de Potrancas for fillies (both staged in September), October's Group One Premio Nacional Ricardo Lyon and November's Premio Las Oaks, as well as significant Group One-level prizes.

Like all the major Chilean tracks, Club Hípico has hosted the Gran Premio Latinoamericano, which moves around South America, and is the only venue at which the runners race right-handed.

Away from the racing, the course, which was fortunate to escape serious damage in the devastating Chilean earthquake of 2010, is a popular concert venue in Santiago.

Guayaquil

Ecuador

LOCATION: IN THE BEND BETWEEN TWO RIVERS AT SAMBORONDÓN, AROUND SIX MILES (9.7KM) NORTH OF THE CITY OF GUAYAQUIL

THE TRACK: LEFT-HANDED, OVAL, DIRT TRACK, SEVEN FURLONGS (1,400M); RACING ONCE A WEEK THROUGHOUT THE YEAR, USUALLY ON SUNDAYS

PRINCIPAL RACES: CLÁSICO DERBY NACIONAL BENJAMIN ROSALES

OPENED: 1980

FAMOUS MOMENTS: MARÍA JOSE JAIME, THE FIRST FEMALE ECUADORIAN JOCKEY, COMPETES AGAINST WOMEN FROM ACROSS THE CONTINENT IN AN INTERNATIONAL COMPETITION AT THE TRACK IN 2013, WHICH WAS WON BY AMERICAN ASHLEY YODICE

Although not Ecuador's capital city, the heaving river port of Guayaquil is the country's largest and most populous conurbation, and its last bastion of racing. There used to be other tracks, but demand for development sites left followers of the turf without an outlet, until a new project got underway, backed by both public and private investment. A largely undeveloped area in rice-growing country was chosen, close to the confluence where the Daule and Babahoyo rivers flow into the mighty Guayas.

The track itself was first known as Hipódromo El Buijo, but only had a brief existence before coming under a new management company in 1984. It is now named Hipódromo Miguel Salem Dibo, after a patrician of the Ecuadorian racing industry.

The watery feel of the area is reflected at the racecourse by a large lake and long grassland in the infield. It is no deserted country track though: it can accommodate 29,000 people and has hosted a few international jockey events. Ecuadorian racegoers are renowned for their boundless enthusiasm for horseracing, as demonstrated by their great cries of '¡Dale, dale!', 'Go, go!'.

Asunción

Paraguay

LOCATION: IN THE CAPITAL CITY, SOUTH OF THE CENTRE

THE TRACK: LEFT-HANDED, OVAL, DIRT OF A MILE AND ONE FURLONG (1,810M) WITH 492-YARD (450M) HOME STRAIGHT; RACES EVERY SUNDAY FROM FEBRUARY TO DECEMBER

PRINCIPAL RACES: PREMIO ESPECIAL PRESIDENTE DE LA REPÚBLICA

OPENED: 1954

It is more than likely that most visitors to the Hipódromo de Tembetary will have not been there for one of its many race meetings. Being one of the biggest open spaces in Asunción, the ancient Spanish colonial capital close to the Argentinian border, it is in much demand when musical superstars hit town. Anyone who is anyone has performed there, from the Colombian songstress Shakira and Justin Bieber to Guns N' Roses.

Run by the Paraguay Jockey Club, it is a sedate and understated place close to a few other sporting institutions. Two modern but low-key grandstands look out onto a hedge-lined green expanse; there is a surprisingly rural feel despite its location along a bustling arterial road. Of particular note is the vivid red colour of the dirt course, and its great width of twenty-two yards (20m).

While horses are very much part of the national identity, and can still often be seen pulling carts in much of the country, the racing is generally of a modest grade.

Monterrico

Peru

LOCATION: FIVE MILES (8KM) SOUTHEAST OF CENTRAL LIMA

THE TRACK: LEFT-HANDED, OVAL, DIRT CIRCUIT OF A MILE AND ONE FURLONG (1,800M) WITH TURF OVAL INSIDE; RACES USUALLY FOUR TIMES A WEEK THROUGHOUT THE YEAR, THURSDAY–SUNDAY

PRINCIPAL RACES: DERBY NACIONAL, LATE NOVEMBER/EARLY DECEMBER

OPENED: 1960

FAMOUS MOMENTS: THE $500,000 PRIZE FOR THE 2014 GRAN PREMIO LATINOAMERICANO, WON ON HOME SOIL BY LIDERIS, MAKES IT THE RICHEST RACE EVER HELD ON THE CONTINENT

There were a number of other incarnations of racecourses in Lima before the arrival of Monterrico in 1960. Because of its prime, central location and position next to, of all things, Peru's largest and busiest department store – the appropriately named Jockey Plaza – as well as its proximity to the huge American Embassy and the University, it is perhaps surprising that it has not been moved again.

It seems there has been an appreciation that people would stop attending if the country's only thoroughbred course moved out into the sticks, and when the previous venue at nearby San Felipe became so popular that it outgrew its location, the Peruvian Jockey Club obtained this land instead for what was a very expensive development back in the late 1950s.

Monterrico is not the prettiest of tracks. The large stands are functional with a fairly industrial backdrop and shabby-looking infield, but it is well promoted, free to enter, offers high-quality racing, and the crowds do come. At other times, music acts from Morrissey to Katy Perry have performed concerts here.

There is a substantial statue in honour of the country's thoroughbred icon Santorin, who in 1973 became the first to win the 'Quadruple Crown' of Monterrico's major races, plus the hugely prestigious Gran Premio Carlos Pellegrini in Buenos Aires by thirteen lengths. Santorin, said to be the 'saviour of Peruvian racing', was taken to Florida the following year for an attempt at valuable races at Hialeah Park, but never seemed his old self; he later became an influential stallion back home. Just as Santorin's trainer Juan Suarez was breaking new ground, his son, also Juan, followed the family tradition when his champion mare Almudena became the first Peruvian horse to race at the Breeders' Cup.

Breeding is a rich person's game, yet there seem to be plenty involved to keep the nation's bloodstock industry in robust health, including former Bayern Munich and Chelsea striker Claudio Pizarro, who bred Almudena. The industry's pinnacle so far came via Empery, victor of the 1976 Epsom Derby under Lester Piggott; the colt's dam was Peruvian Triple Crown-winner Pamploma.

Many jockeys have started off in Lima's jockeys' academy and ended up making a mark when emigrating to America. They include Edgar Prado, Jorge Chavez, Jose Valdivia Jr and Rafael Bejarano.

Montevideo

Uruguay

LOCATION: HIPÓDROMO NACIONAL DE MAROÑAS, IN THE SUBURB OF ITUZAINGÓ, LESS THAN FIVE MILES (8KM) FROM CENTRAL MONTEVIDEO
THE TRACK: LEFT-HANDED, OVAL, DIRT, CIRCUIT OF JUST OVER ONE AND A QUARTER MILES (2,065M)
PRINCIPAL RACES: GRAN PREMIO JOSÉ PEDRO RAMÍREZ, JANUARY; PERIODICALLY HOST TO THE GRAN PREMIO LATINOAMERICANO

OPENED: 1874
FAMOUS MOMENTS: SCENE OF A FAILED ASSASSINATION ATTEMPT ON PRESIDENT GABRIEL TERRA, 1935

Maroñas may be located in the less than salubrious Ituzaingó district of the Uruguayan capital, but to see it anyone could be forgiven for thinking it was in one of the most exclusive. The large, art deco entrance has a distinctly palatial feel to it, and the buildings, extensively renovated for the 2003 re-opening after five years of closure, are beautifully maintained.

The shutters came down as a result of financial problems, which became so acute that horses and jockeys were competing against each other with no prize money on offer.

The first horseracing on the site was in 1874, and the somewhat rickety early viewing area was replaced in 1888 by a much grander structure.

Uruguay prides itself on being a nation of horse lovers, and none has filled their affections more than the Argentinian-bred Invasor, winner of the colts' Triple Crown at Maroñas in 2005. The horse was subsequently purchased by Sheikh Hamdan al Maktoum of Dubai, for whom he won the Breeders' Cup Classic (2006) and the Dubai World Cup (2007). Uruguayans followed his every step, and when he returned to the country to become a stallion, he was welcomed like a national hero at Maroñas.

Caracas

Venezuela

LOCATION: ABOUT FIVE MILES (8KM) SOUTHWEST OF CENTRAL CARACAS

THE TRACK: LEFT-HANDED, OVAL, DIRT TRACK OF A MILE AND ONE FURLONG (1,800M) WITH A SPRINT CHUTE; MEETINGS EVERY SATURDAY AND SUNDAY THROUGHOUT THE YEAR

PRINCIPAL RACES: CLÁSICO SIMÓN BOLÍVAR, OCTOBER

OPENED: 1959

FAMOUS MOMENTS: CANONERO II, A BARGAIN BUY AND APPARENT NO-HOPER WITH CROOKED LEGS FROM AMERICA, WINNING HIS DEBUT RACE AT LA RINCONADA IN 1970 BEFORE CAUSING A MASSIVE KENTUCKY DERBY SHOCK A YEAR LATER

Built to replace the previous Caracas racecourse, which had outgrown its central location, La Rinconada Hippodrome was unveiled as one of the most magnificent tracks not only in South America, but in the world. It cost $80 million even in the 1950s, another of the lavish projects of military dictator General Pérez Jiménez, which also included a replica of the Rockefeller Center.

Jiménez had fled the country by the time La Rinconada opened; at least his racing legacy was not only striking, but the facilities also helped to revive the industry. Vast stands, designed by the famed American racecourse architect Arthur Froehlich, were constructed along with landscaped gardens. The setting is framed, like most of Caracas, by mountains.

There are regular stories about gambling corruption in the city. Nonetheless, there is a high standard of racing, and lots of it: it is not unusual to see twenty racecards. Since jockey Gustavo Ávila broke into America aboard Canonero II, the likes of Javier Castellano and Ramón Domínguez have followed to become very successful Stateside riders.

Casablanca-Anfa

Ngong

Borrowdale Park

Champ de Mars

Greyville

Kenilworth

Africa

Ngong

Kenya

LOCATION: SEVEN AND A HALF MILES (12KM) WEST OF NAIROBI CITY CENTRE

THE TRACK: RIGHT-HANDED, OVAL, TURF JUST UNDER TWO MILES (2400M); ELEVEN-MONTH SEASON FROM AUGUST TO JULY

PRINCIPAL RACES: KENYA DERBY, APRIL

OPENED: 1954

Ngong, the only racecourse in East Africa, stages fixtures on Sundays during the season. Home for the Ngong Racecourse and Golf Park, run by the Jockey Club of Kenya, has been the attractive, tree-lined course at Ngong since the 1950s, when Nairobi's track at Kariokor was sold for development.

Officials had the wide-open spaces of Ascot racecourse in the UK in mind when they designed the course – where the runners also have plenty of room to spread out – though the circuit is oval as opposed to Ascot's more triangular layout.

With so much dry, hot weather, ground conditions can become very firm, and an irrigation system has been constructed for both the horseracing track and the nine-hole golf course in the middle.

British settlers started racing in Kenya at the turn of the twentieth century, and the sport gained a reputation for catering only for the white elite. However, the Jockey Club of Kenya has gone out of its way to encourage a mixed membership in an effort to ensure the sport survives.

Although there is a small thoroughbred breeding industry in Kenya, many of the horses are imported from South Africa, and are trained on the track at Ngong.

Versions of all the traditional Classic races are staged including, for a century, the Kenya Derby in April.

Champn de Mars

Mauritius

LOCATION: IN PORT LOUIS, THE CAPITAL OF MAURITIUS

THE TRACK: RIGHT-HANDED, OVAL, VERY NARROW, TURF CIRCUIT OF SIX AND A HALF FURLONGS (1,298M), 273-YARD (250M) HOME STRAIGHT; RACING BETWEEN MARCH AND DECEMBER

PRINCIPAL RACES: MAIDEN CUP, SEPTEMBER

OPENED: 1812

FAMOUS MOMENTS: ANNUAL INTERNATIONAL JOCKEYS' CHALLENGE

The racecourse at Champ de Mars is believed to be the oldest organised venue in the Southern Hemisphere, having been in existence since 1812. Prior to this, the Indian Ocean island of Mauritius had been ruled for a century by the French as the 'Isle de France', and held significant strategic importance during the Napoleonic Wars. Despite being captured by British forces in 1810, the island remained to all intents and purposes French, and horseracing was seen as a pleasant way to encourage more cordial relations between the two sides.

The racecourse is tiny, right in Port Louis, crammed in between the urban sprawl and the foothills of Signal Mountain. This location only adds to the frenetic atmosphere generated by noisy, betting-mad punters and the bookmakers.

The Mauritius Turf Club stages the fixtures – some consisting of as many as fifteen races – including the historic Group One Maiden Cup in September over a mile and a half (2,400m).

Around a dozen trainers are responsible for 340 horses at the stables. The horses, many of which originate from South Africa, are monitored closely by officials before their races, following claims of corruption over the years. The island also possesses world-renowned laboratory facilities for dope-testing.

The season starts with the Group Two Duchess of York Stakes which, together with the Group One Duke of York Cup, recalls a visit by the Duke and Duchess – later King George VI and Queen Elizabeth – in 1927. Since 1984, the season has ended with the two-day International Jockeys' Weekend, which proves as popular with racegoers as with the riders, who jet in keen to relax on the holiday island as well as take part in the races.

Casablanca-Anfa

Morocco

LOCATION: IN THE FASHIONABLE DISTRICT OF ANFA, WEST OF CENTRAL CASABLANCA

THE TRACK: RIGHT-HANDED, OVAL, DIRT TRACK OF A LITTLE OVER A MILE (1,700M); MEETINGS EVERY FRIDAY BETWEEN SEPTEMBER AND JULY

PRINCIPAL RACES: GRAND PRIX SA MAJESTÉ LE ROI MOHAMMED, NOVEMBER

OPENED: 1912

It is dispiriting to hear of the many nations in which racing is crumbling after decades of popularity. So, it is somewhat reassuring to learn that the sport appears to be going from strength to strength in Morocco. There are half a dozen tracks and plans for more, with around 1,800 races spread between those for thoroughbreds, purebred Arabians, the Anglo-Arabian developed mostly in France, and the speedy local Barb horses, which played a part in the breeding of the thoroughbred.

Casablanca, or Casa-Anfa as it is generally known, is the oldest racecourse and the country's most important, holding a number of the feature races, including a more recently introduced Meeting International du Maroc each November. The fixture offers more than €625,000 in prize money – impressive purses for any jurisdiction in the world – and while it has not caught the imagination of all the key racing nations because of the competition and the time of year, plenty of generally second-tier horses from the likes of France and Spain have made the journey.

Progress in Moroccan racing has been driven by the establishment of the Société Royale d'Encouragement du Cheval (SOREC) in 2003, a government-appointed organisation which has been modernising and promoting the breeding and racing industry and forging a link with the French Pari Mutuel Urbain (PMU). The races are held under French rules.

Many tourists, aside from those romantic aficionados of Humphrey Bogart's eponymous 1942 classic film, spurn Morocco's most populous city in favour of Marrakesh or Tangiers, but amid the chaos of Casablanca's businesses and diverse architectural styles, this neat little racecourse provides some breathing space. Not too far from the beach and the famous Corniche area, it is fringed by palm trees and has a nine-hole golf course in the middle. A grandstand, with 700 seats, is decorated with the national colours of red and green.

While most of the thoroughbreds, apart from talented French export Billabong, have made limited impact, the Arabians have done better. They not only win the local races in May's Arabian International Racing Day, but also events as far afield as Britain. The key player has been Sharif El Alami and his Jalobey Stud near Rabat, which retained respected French trainer Jean de Roualle for a few years.

Greyville

South Africa

LOCATION: ONE AND A HALF MILES (2.4KM) NORTHWEST OF CENTRAL DURBAN

THE TRACK: RIGHT-HANDED, UNDULATING, PEAR-SHAPED, TURF TRACK OF A MILE AND THREE-QUARTERS (2,800M) WITH POLYTRACK CIRCUIT INSIDE; MEETINGS HELD THROUGHOUT THE YEAR, INCLUDING UNDER FLOODLIGHTS

PRINCIPAL RACES: DURBAN JULY

OPENED: 1896

There is glitz and glamour at showpiece racing fixtures around the world, but few do it quite like the people of Durban. The Durban July fixture attracts crowds of 50,000 and some of the most vibrant and original costumes you will see, matching a theme such as 'the colour of magic' or 'the leader of the pack'.

Aside from the fashion and assorted entertainment, a significant race is taking place. The Durban July, although a handicap, rivals Kenilworth's Sun Met as South Africa's most important race. Sizeable prize money means that the best middle-distance performers in the country will often try to run in both – horses

like London News and the redoubtable Power Pocket, who completed the double in the same year, 2008.

Greyville is squeezed into its central spot, close to Durban's famous Golden Mile promenade, and its location has caused some problems. An underpass was constructed to ease traffic, which has resulted in undulating sections around the track before it leads into a level home straight of two furlongs (400m). In the middle of the racecourse is the Royal Durban Golf Club, which has been around just as long and is one of only four in the country to have earned the lofty prefix courtesy of King George V. It is of championship standard, having even hosted a teenaged Nick Faldo in the 1975 Commonwealth Tournament.

There are many other Group-level races in the calendar, at what is one of the nation's premier tracks, with the artificial Polytrack course added in 2014, and supplying Friday night floodlit meetings for half of the year, away from the intense daytime heat of KwaZulu-Natal.

The Durban July, however, is what makes it all tick. Famously, there have been several coincidence winners, including in 1960, when horse number 13 Left Wing won the race a week after Hennie van Zyl, wearing the number 13 jersey, scored both tries for the Springboks in a 13-0 defeat of the New Zealand All Blacks. And in 2004, as South Africa celebrated 10 years of democracy, it was decided all number 10 saddlecloths in races would be adorned with the national flag. It probably does not need telling which number the winner Greys Inn was carrying.

Kenilworth
South Africa

LOCATION: IN THE CAPE TOWN SUBURB OF KENILWORTH, NINE MILES (14.5KM) SOUTHEAST OF THE CENTRE

THE TRACK: LEFT-HANDED, ROUND, TURF; 'NEW' COURSE OF ONE AND THREE-QUARTER MILES (2,800M) WITH THREE-FURLONG (600M) HOME STRAIGHT, 'OLD' COURSE OF A MILE AND TWO THIRDS (2,700M) WITH 492-YARD (450M) HOME STRAIGHT, UNDULATING SPRINT STRAIGHT OF SIX FURLONGS (1,200M); RACING OCTOBER–FEBRUARY

PRINCIPAL RACES: THE CAPE METROPOLITAN STAKES, JANUARY; THE QUEEN'S PLATE, JANUARY

OPENED: 1881

Kenilworth racecourse has a bit of everything: Africa's richest race-day, stunning views of Table Mountain, and one of the most important managed botanical sites in the world. The Kenilworth Racecourse Conservation Area in the centre of the track consists of 130 acres of scrubland and wetland containing hundreds of plant species, some of them endangered.

On the surrounding track, the historic 'Met' is the centrepiece. A handicap, it is run as one of twelve races on a bumper card in late January and staged over a mile and a quarter (2,000m) of Kenilworth's sizeable circuit. A major social occasion for Capetonians, with as many as 50,000 people attending, the Met has been won by some of South African racing's foremost stars including the grey Wolf Power (1984), London News (1997), the brilliant Horse Chestnut (1999) and three-time winner Pocket Power (2007–2009).

London News added the race to Kenilworth's Queen's Plate, which he won a month earlier before going on to success in the Queen Elizabeth II Cup at Sha Tin in China that April. Two months later, the South African flag-bearer was in the UK, finishing third in the Prince of Wales's Stakes at Royal Ascot. In his three-year-old season, Horse Chestnut – like London News, bred in South Africa – won the Triple Crown and ran away with the Met as the first of his age group to claim success in fifty years. He briefly raced on in America before injury forced retirement to stud as perhaps South Africa's greatest and most popular racehorse.

As well as the Met, other Kenilworth highlights include the Queen's Plate, which also takes place in January, the Cape Guineas races (December) and, again in January, the Cape Derby.

Having hogged the headlines in the Met for three years, Pocket Power was even more dominant in the Queen's Plate, staged over one mile (1,600m). A real favourite at Kenilworth where he was only ever defeated once over the one-mile distance, the horse gained huge popularity with the public as he took the Queen's Plate an unprecedented four times between 2006 and 2010.

Borrowdale Park

Zimbabwe

LOCATION: IN THE UPMARKET SUBURB OF BORROWDALE, SIX MILES (9.7KM) NORTH OF CENTRAL HARARE

THE TRACK: RIGHT-HANDED, GALLOPING, OVAL, TURF COURSE OF A MILE AND THREE-QUARTERS (2,800M); MEETINGS HELD JANUARY–JULY AND SEPTEMBER–DECEMBER, USUALLY ON SUNDAYS

PRINCIPAL RACES: ZIMBABWE DERBY, LATE APRIL/EARLY MAY

OPENED: 1958

FAMOUS MOMENTS: LOCALLY BRED IPI TOMBE WON FOUR OF HER FIRST FIVE STARTS AT BORROWDALE BEFORE A TRANSFER TO SOUTH AFRICA AND THEN RACES IN DUBAI AND THE US

It is no surprise to learn that Zimbabwe's last racecourse, following the closure of Bulawayo in 2001, has been affected by a country riven by political upheaval. Introduced under the Mashonaland Turf Club in 1892, racing used to be the preserve of the white minority, yet its popularity amongst all has helped it to survive. Unfortunately, the downward economic spiral of the Mugabe years had a knock-on effect at the racecourse, with no money for punters to spend and horse numbers dwindling alarmingly. Local horses are easy prey for South African raiders at each fixture.

There have been regular concerns that the track will close, but public interest remains as do decent crowds, no doubt boosted by musical acts and cheaper lager available on Castle Tankard day in April. The brewery has been allied with this mile-and-a-quarter (2,000m) event since 1960, making it the oldest sponsored race in Africa.

Certainly, the turf is not as pristine as it was, and facilities are becoming increasingly antiquated, but hopes exist that there is now light at the end of the tunnel.

Asia

Riffa

Bahrain

LOCATION: JUST SOUTH OF RIFFA, THE KINGDOM'S SECOND BIGGEST CITY, IN THE CENTRE OF THE ISLAND

THE TRACK: RIGHT-HANDED, TRIANGULAR TURF TRACK OF A MILE AND A HALF (2,400M) WITH SAND TRACK INSIDE; FIXTURES EVERY FRIDAY, OCTOBER–APRIL

PRINCIPAL RACES: CROWN PRINCE CUP, FEBRUARY; KING'S CUP, MARCH

OPENED: 1981

Although only an independent nation since 1971, the history of racing in this small island kingdom stretches back much further. The ruling Al Khalifa family have bred and raced Arabian horses for several centuries, and there used to be private challenges held at a small venue closer to the capital city, Manama.

There is now just the one track, very close to the Grand Prix motor racing circuit. It is home to 300 horses, enough to fill the six races scheduled per week. One is usually dedicated to Arabians, and the thoroughbred events divided between imported horses and the local-breds. Bahrain has its own registered stud books and a number of its own stallions.

They have made the best of the Rashid Equestrian & Horse Racing Club, which is not exactly picturesque. There is a lake in the infield, but the scrubby surrounding landscape gives way to industrial plants associated with producing oil and aluminium, Bahrain's most important exports.

As is the case of other Arabian nations, the sport in Bahrain is underpinned by the interest of the ruling family, and its king and crown prince have been known to attend meetings. The 3,000-capacity grandstand can be full on major days, but gambling is prohibited in the kingdom. Lucrative prizes ensure that big-name jockeys jet in on occasions, and expatriates, such as Allan Smith, a former British jockey, and James Naylor, have carved out good livings as local trainers. Well-travelled British-born riders Gary Hind and Brett Doyle have also continued their careers on the island.

Keen to promote itself worldwide, the Kingdom of Bahrain sponsors British racing's Group One fillies race, the Sun Chariot Stakes, at Newmarket in the autumn. With the steady investment in the racing, Bahrain-trained horses have done well overseas. Successful businessman and owner Fawzi Nass has invested in his own stable, as well as a stud and satellite yard in Newmarket. The undoubted star so far for Nass has been Krypton Factor, winner of the 2012 Golden Shaheen on Dubai World Cup night and sixth that year behind Black Caviar in the Diamond Jubilee Stakes at Royal Ascot. Another wealthy investor, Jaber Ramadhan, has also enjoyed success in Dubai after launching his Bahrain-based training project.

Happy Valley

China

LOCATION: HONG KONG ISLAND

THE TRACK: RIGHT-HANDED, OVAL, TURF CIRCUIT OF JUST UNDER A MILE (1,450M) WITH CHUTE, 339-YARD (310M) HOME STRAIGHT; FIXTURES MAINLY ON WEDNESDAY NIGHTS, SEPTEMBER–JULY

PRINCIPAL RACES: JANUARY CUP

OPENED: 1846

FAMOUS MOMENTS: ANNUAL INTERNATIONAL JOCKEYS' CHAMPIONSHIP

The racecourse at Happy Valley has gained almost iconic status for its city location in a bowl of skyscrapers to the north, east and south, with Mount Cameron to the southwest. A playground for locals, it typically hosts race meetings on Wednesday evenings.

The track and area's beginnings were not as salubrious and picturesque as racegoers see today, however. It was originally a British naval base, but its location on a malaria-ridden swamp led to a considerable number of deaths, so it was abandoned. In 1841, a naval commander named William Brodie was buried there during the First Opium War and it became known as 'Happy Valley', a place for 'eternal happiness'. The racecourse took the name of the cemetery that still overlooks it to this day, though that is now formally named 'Hong Kong Cemetery'.

Nevertheless, the British decided it was the only place horseracing could be run on Hong Kong Island (everyone had to travel to Macau before) so the swamp was drained and the racing began, typically just once a year, from 1846. It wasn't until 1884 that the Hong Kong Jockey Club was formalised and 1971 when the administration switched from an amateur to a professional organisation.

The idea that Happy Valley racecourse is cursed perseveres as a superstition for some local racegoers. In 1918, the temporary grandstand caught fire and collapsed on Derby day, killing 600 people. More recently, luck was on the side of the racecourse when an audacious attempt to apparently fix races with an elaborate poison dart system was uncovered in 2007. Located at the three-quarters-of-a-mile (1,200m) start, a remote operating device was designed to trigger the poison darts into the horses' underbellies as they passed. Local gangsters were suspected of being responsible for the conspiracy.

Since 1978, all of Hong Kong's most important races have moved to the newly developed course at Sha Tin. The January Cup, inaugurated in 2012, is Happy Valley's only current graded race, but it has been won by internationally recognised stars such as Military Attack, a future Queen Elizabeth II Cup winner and Hong Kong Horse of the Year in 2013. The biggest event on Happy Valley's calendar is the International Jockeys' Championship – the richest of its kind – run in December on the Wednesday before the major Sha Tin international meeting.

Sha Tin

China

LOCATION: NEW TERRITORIES, TWELVE MILES (19.3KM) FROM CENTRAL DISTRICT, HONG KONG

THE TRACK: RIGHT-HANDED, OVAL, LEVEL WITH CHUTES; TURF TRACK OF NINE AND A HALF FURLONGS (1,900M) WITH 470-YARD (430M) HOME STRAIGHT; ALL-WEATHER TRACK OF ALMOST ONE MILE (1,560M) WITH STRAIGHT OF 400 YARDS (365M); RACING FROM SEPTEMBER TO JULY

PRINCIPAL RACES: HONG KONG INTERNATIONAL RACES, DECEMBER

OPENED: 1978

FAMOUS MOMENTS: SILENT WITNESS WINS SECOND HONG KONG SPRINT, 2004

The comparatively new circuit at Sha Tin has become an internationally renowned racecourse in a very short time. Built on reclaimed land, it stages fixtures mainly on Sundays during the season.

Surrounded by high-rise blocks, and with crowds of up to around 100,000, its atmosphere is famously frenetic and betting turns over more than HK$1 billion each time. With space a premium in Hong Kong, Sha Tin houses all of the current horses in training, and the track is abuzz every morning with the equine community.

Unsurprisingly, there is no breeding programme – though plans are afoot to try to make room – and all horses are imported. Local owners enjoy officially renaming their charges, often giving them names in Chinese that are not necessarily comparable in translation to English; hence, Everyday Lettuce and What Man Horse have raced. The words 'Dragon', 'Lucky' and 'Win' feature prominently in horses' monikers. Retiring stars cannot stay in Hong Kong either, so the Hong Kong Jockey Club organises parties for locals to bid farewell to their racing legends.

One of the most famous stars was Silent Witness, who currently resides in the equine retirement village of Living Legends in Melbourne, Australia. He won seventeen sprint races on the trot between 2003 and 2005, including a string of Group One races against international opposition. His popularity was so great that, when the Club gave away Silent Witness commemorative caps to the crowd in 2005, his passionate followers caused a trampling incident in which twenty-one racegoers were injured.

The biggest jockey star of the modern age is Brazilian-born João Moreira, the 'Magic Man'. His domination of the Hong Kong racing scene was most apparent when he won a record eight of the eleven Sha Tin races in March 2017. Moreira also built up a tremendous rapport with Able Friend, Hong Kong's Horse of the Year in 2015. That season, the horse, already the highest internationally ranked Hong Kong horse in history, won five races at Sha Tin, and only finished outside the first three once all year, when he travelled to the UK for Royal Ascot.

International eyes are drawn to the New Territories track in mid-December, when it hosts the Hong Kong International Races: the Cup, Vase, Mile and Sprint. An array of international talent gives the event a seal of approval by showing up at Sha Tin. Victorious travellers have included Ireland's Highland Reel and Japan's Maurice, France's Flintshire, Britain's Snow Fairy, and New Zealand's Sunline.

Taipa

China

LOCATION: AT THE NORTHERN END OF TAIPA, THE ISLAND
CONNECTED TO MAINLAND MACAU BY ROAD BRIDGE
THE TRACK: FLOODLIT, RIGHT-HANDED, OVAL TURF OF A MILE (1,600M),
WITH 405-YARD (370M) HOME STRAIGHT; INSIDE SAND TRACK OF SEVEN
FURLONGS (1,400M), WITH 350-YARD (320M) STRAIGHT; TWICE-A-WEEK
FIXTURES ALL YEAR ROUND

PRINCIPAL RACES: MACAU HONG KONG TROPHY, MARCH;
MACAU DERBY, APRIL
OPENED: 1989 AFTER A SPELL AS A TROTTING TRACK

The reason most people head to Macau, the tiny former Portuguese colony in China, is for the gambling. The vast casinos litter this 'Asian Las Vegas', and there has been a racecourse at different times and locations here since the eighteenth century.

Essentially, though, visitors' priorities tend to be more on the tables and machines than the horses, and there was an absence of racing for 30 years before this venue appeared, close to the Pearl River Estuary and the small international airport. They tried trotting for a decade, to general public apathy, before laying down a dirt course for thoroughbreds, and a turf track a year later. A four-storey grandstand with a capacity of 15,000 soon came to fruition, with a formal Jockey Club organisation and its own set of rules.

For a few years in the 1990s it thrived and became quite a fashionable destination, with its floodlights, well-maintained infield complete with lake, and views of both mountains and cityscape. However, times have not been so equable lately. Facilities have become shabby and there have been allegations that the operators have been running at a loss, and that the stabling facilities are not entirely up to scratch. The horse population has dwindled

alarmingly, raising fears for the future, but major investment has been promised.

Macau is certainly the poorer cousin of Hong Kong, in terms of quality racing. These two Special Administrative Regions of China sometimes compete their horses in Interport competitions, as they are only a 55-minute ferry ride apart, with Hong Kong runners invariably the stronger.

In Taipa's brief history, Australians have made the most impact, both in terms of imported horses and in the saddle. Jockey John Didham dominated in the mid-1990s, while Gary Moore, a one-time champion jockey and Prix de l'Arc de Triomphe winner in France, and Hong Kong champion too, trained here for thirteen years before leaving in 2014.

Moore ended up in Macau as he had become something of a persona non grata across the water in Hong Kong after the infamous 'Shanghai Syndicate' race-fixing scandal of the 1980s, which had seen him suspended. He was known for kissing victorious jockeys excitedly, and even jumping onto their horses in celebration.

Nicosia

Cyprus

LOCATION: IN THE SUBURB OF AGIOS DOMETIOS, WEST OF NICOSIA

THE TRACK: LEFT-HANDED, LEFT-HANDED, EGG SHAPED, SIX AND
A HALF FURLONGS (1300M)

PRINCIPAL RACES: CYPRUS DERBY, NOVEMBER

OPENED: 1878

Horseracing in its modern form came to Cyprus in the late nineteenth century as a result of British soldiers and local police testing their horses against each other.

The track is dotted with royal palms, eucalyptus trees, other greenery and terraces, and the view towards the Kyrenia Mountains is striking and often colourful, leading the *Sporting Life* newspaper to once describe the course as 'the most picturesque in the world'. Facilities, which underwent renovations in the late 1990s, remain stylish, and the course is a popular destination.

The Nicosia Race Club is scheduled to stage fixtures of up to ten races at the island's sole course, any of which are cancelled if insufficient runners are entered. The Cyprus Turf Club enforces the rules. Feature of the year is the Cyprus Derby staged for only modest prize money, illustrating that finances can be challenging.

There have been several whiffs of subterfuge in Cypriot racing: a British-born official and campaigner against corruption was shot at while driving in Nicosia in 2016, which led to racing being briefly cancelled.

Bangalore

India

LOCATION: IN THE CENTRE OF THE SOUTHEAST INDIAN CITY

THE TRACK: RIGHT-HANDED, UNDULATING, OVAL TURF COURSE OF A LITTLE UNDER A MILE AND A QUARTER (1,950M); MEETINGS HELD DURING WINTER AND SUMMER SEASONS

PRINCIPAL RACES: BANGALORE DERBY, FEBRUARY

OPENED: 1921

FAMOUS MOMENTS: BRITISH JOCKEY DAVID ALLAN BECOMES THE MOST SUCCESSFUL FOREIGN RIDER IN INDIAN RACING HISTORY WHEN LANDING HIS TWENTY-THIRD CLASSIC IN THE 2018 BANGALORE 2000 GUINEAS, PASSING THE RECORD OF SANDY BARCLAY

They take their racing seriously in Bangalore (now officially called Bengaluru); in fact, perhaps too seriously. So passionate and angry do punters become that there was an all-out riot in 2013. When the stewards decided to amend the result of a race after objections and a half-hour inquiry, racegoers threw chairs and bottles around and smashed television screens, causing the rest of the day's action to be cancelled. Other scenes have prompted officials to erect a metal fence between the paddock and the racecourse, in order for jockeys to feel safe when results have gone against the crowd.

Many of the important races are held in the winter season during January and February. There has long been a tradition of European riders spending a spell in the country – British champion-turned-trainer Richard Hughes was a high-profile regular – but that has been affected by racecourse incidents and the growth of racing in the Far East and UAE. Top names continue to fly in for the Bangalore features, when crowds of more than 20,000 cram into the tight premises, with the well-dressed cream of high society parading in the smarter enclosures.

Every corner of the Bangalore Turf Club is used. Set in just 85 acres, it somehow accommodates more than 1,000 stables, which peer over the side of the track along with grand old buildings. There is even a swimming pool, veterinary hospital and jockey school. It must feel a long way away from the old days of the British Raj, when this was a land of polo and gymkhanas. The course was even dug up during a military occupation in the Second World War.

The committee is proud of its history, and application to become a member of the Club is extremely sought after. With a largely pleasant climate, it has a strong standard of racing with plenty of established prizes; business magnates Cyrus Poonawalla and Vijay Mallya are amongst those regularly enjoying success. However, the form does not always translate: the 2016 St Leger winner Desert God made little impression when transferred to Hughes in the UK and tried in basement-level British events.

Internal politics has caused problems in recent years, with fierce disagreements about betting licences and police investigation into rigged races. The decision by the Indian government to withdraw several banknotes from circulation in 2017 caused such chaos that bookmakers could not operate, and meetings were cancelled.

Kolkata

India

LOCATION: IN THE MAIDAN, A VAST PARK IN THE CITY, ON THE BANKS OF THE HUGLI RIVER

THE TRACK: LARGE, RIGHT-HANDED, OVAL TURF COURSE OF JUST UNDER A MILE AND THREE-QUARTERS (2,800M), WITH ANOTHER GRASS COURSE AND TRAINING TRACK INSIDE; MEETINGS FROM JULY TO MARCH

PRINCIPAL RACES: KOLKATA DERBY, JANUARY

OPENED: 1812

FAMOUS MOMENTS: QUEEN ELIZABETH AND PRINCE PHILIP PRESENTING THE FIRST QUEEN ELIZABETH II CUP; A NEW TROPHY IS SENT FROM BUCKINGHAM PALACE EACH YEAR

Traditionalists would perhaps be taken aback by any reference to Kolkata racecourse. This, after all, is the Royal Calcutta Turf Club, with some two centuries of history. The regal title was added after King George V made his second visit to the races in 1912. It remains a powerful reminder of the British Empire, with all the trappings of the times. The green space upon which it sits is a legacy of the historic traders of the East India Company, and was originally a parade ground. It is a vital, grassy leisure facility, also home to many games of amateur cricket, with the iconic Eden Gardens stadium at the opposite end to the racecourse. As this is still army land, it contains the barracks and polo club, as well as a zoo and the picturesque Elliot Park. Overlooking the racecourse, as well as most of The Maidan, is Victoria Memorial, a marble palace built in memory of Queen Victoria.

Other places in the city were used for horseracing until this location was selected in 1812; races were held in the mornings until 1876, when it was decided that afternoons were rather more suitable. It is a vast place, with four grandstands tracing back to around 1905. Meetings certainly have a throwback feel to them, with military bands often playing and English commentary. The paddock is surrounded by trees, offering valuable shade to spectators.

The racing is of a decent standard, with Kolkata having a strong rivalry with Bangalore to stage the best action; each has its own series of Classic races. At Kolkata, there are two separate 'monsoon' and 'cold weather' seasons, although the racing is almost year-round, and the track is free-draining.

All the racing nowadays is on the flat, but jump racing used to be popular and, until 1929, a Grand National was staged. The last winner, the Gertrude Hartley-owned Kilbuck, went on to run in the Aintree Grand National in 1931 (fell at the last fence) and 1934 (refused). Hartley's husband, Ernest, was a steward and their only daughter was to become rather better known as the actress Vivien Leigh.

Records indicate a staging of the Derby in 1844, and that race remains the most important event today.

Mahalaxmi

India

LOCATION: ELEVEN MILES (17.7KM) SOUTHWEST OF THE CENTRE OF
MUMBAI
THE TRACK: RIGHT-HANDED, OVAL, TURF, ONE AND A HALF MILES
(2,400M); RACING FROM NOVEMBER TO APRIL
PRINCIPAL RACES: INDIAN DERBY, FEBRUARY
OPENED: 1883

FAMOUS MOMENTS: PESI SHROFF ADDS TRAINING THE WINNER OF THE
INDIAN DERBY (2010) TO HIS ACHIEVEMENTS RIDING IN THE RACE

Being located on the largest expanse of greenery in the city, the racecourse at Mahalaxmi has been called the 'lungs of Mumbai'. Set in 225 acres in south Mumbai, and overlooking the sea, it could hardly present more of a contrast to the high-rise blocks and other buildings around it. When there is no racing, the racetrack and its surroundings are a popular recreational destination with Mumbaikars.

Fixtures are staged by the Royal Western India Turf Club, which was formed from the Bombay Turf Club in 1864 and 'made' Royal by King George V in 1935. All of them are held on turf, which has to be regularly watered because of Mumbai's extreme temperatures. Thursdays and Sundays are the usual times for the meetings, and races in the evening, under floodlights, have been introduced to woo a younger audience who work during the day. Mahalaxmi stages Classic races along the traditional model, which were introduced in the 1940s, with the one-and-a-half-mile (2,400m) Indian Derby taking place in early February.

Champion jockey Pesi Shroff is the most successful Derby rider, with eight wins before his retirement from the saddle in 2004. As well as his success, Shroff, who subsequently turned to training, gained a reputation as one of Indian racing's most charismatic riders. This was perhaps never better illustrated than when he had the choice of six mounts in the 1990 Indian Derby: his choice – Star Fire Girl – was a surprise to pundits and followers alike, but the horse duly stormed home to victory.

Shroff became the first person to first ride and subsequently train the big-race winner when the filly Jacqueline, ridden by Britain's three-time champion jockey Richard Hughes, took the prize in 2010. British and Irish riders have been regular sights on the lucrative Indian racing circuits during the European winter, and although some continue to go, others have been put off by a number of controversial decisions by stewards.

At Mahalaxmi, a new club house was opened in 2009, and the Members Stand restored after damage from a fire. And while concerns over the lease on the land on which it operates are no longer seen as a critical issue, changes to tax arrangements have dealt a blow to the finances of all of India's nine courses, and challenging times lie ahead.

Ooty

India

LOCATION: CENTRAL OOTY, A TOWN IN THE NILGIRI HILLS, FIFTY-THREE MILES (85.3KM) NORTH OF COIMBATORE IN SOUTHERN INDIA

THE TRACK: RIGHT-HANDED, OVAL, TURF OF JUST UNDER A MILE AND A QUARTER (2,000M); MEETINGS HELD BETWEEN APRIL AND JUNE

PRINCIPAL RACES: NILGIRI GOLD CUP, MAY

OPENED: 1886

There is not a prettier racecourse in the country than this charming hill station track, with its old blue and white stands and the backdrop of India's Blue Mountains. It is a place to step back in time, with its steam-powered railway – a UNESCO World Heritage site – and tea plantations, reliant on the tourists who arrive for its cool climate and unspoilt forest scenery.

The racecourse, India's only one at high altitude, has only a short season and most of the horses and competitors arrive from its larger sister track in Chennai – both come under the auspices of the Madras Race Club. It is set in just 55 acres and looks a little higgledy-piggledy from up close, with the houses perched on the slopes above almost threatening to topple over onto it.

The state of Tamil Nadu operates strict rules on betting and this came to a head in the mid-1970s when racing was banned for moral reasons. After a decade of stand-offs, Ooty has resumed its popularity as the government acknowledged that racing was a game of skill rather than gambling.

Hanshin

Japan

LOCATION: ADJACENT TO THE MUKO RIVER IN THE CITY OF TAKARAZUKA, FIFTEEN MILES (24.1KM) NORTHWEST OF CENTRAL OSAKA

THE TRACK: TWO PEAR-SHAPED, RIGHT-HANDED GRASS COURSES, THE LARGEST BEING JUST OVER A MILE AND A QUARTER (2,113M), WITH AN ALMOST ONE-MILE (1,518M) DIRT COURSE INSIDE; JUMPS COURSE WHICH BISECTS ITSELF IN THE MIDDLE; MEETINGS ARE HELD ON WEEKENDS THROUGHOUT THE YEAR

PRINCIPAL RACES: OSAKA HAI, APRIL; OKA SHO (JAPANESE 1000 GUINEAS), APRIL; TAKARAZUKA KINEN, JUNE

OPENED: 1948

Along with near neighbour Kyoto, Hanshin is one of the two feature racecourses in Western Japan. It is not far from the Ritto training centre, where half of the country's horses running under the Japanese Racing Association's jurisdiction are based. It was laid out on the site of a factory which manufactured fighter planes in the Second World War. Most of this part of Honshu is very developed, though Takarazuka is quieter than some places, and famed for its theatre and hot-springs resorts.

The racecourse itself is capable of holding 139,000 people. Its grandstand, updated several times already this century, has six floors and is thoughtfully designed with a food plaza, gift shop and fabulous cantilever-roosted paddock.

In a country offering notable interaction between the runners and riders and racegoers, Hanshin's most famous race, the Takarazuka Kinen, is one of two where the field is decided by a public vote. Usually held at the end of June, over a mile and three furlongs (2,200m), it attracts the very best of the middle-distance horses that Japan has spent so long carefully cultivating. Many of the roll-of-honour are household names at home, from Shinzan in 1965 to Tap Dance City some 39 years later.

More recently, with Japanese racing's global ambitions ever-growing, Takarazuka Kinen winners have made an international impression; they include Orfevre, a two-time runner-up in the Prix de l'Arc de Triomphe, notably in 2012, when spectacularly caught in the closing strides, having looked sure of victory. Another of Japan's Arc 'near-misses', Deep Impact, which was third to finish in 2006 but then disqualified after testing positive for a banned substance, won three races from three starts at Hanshin, but his Takarazuka Kinen success was in a year the race was switched to Kyoto. He has subsequently made a major impression as a stallion. The big race was opened to overseas runners in 1997, but precious few have taken up the challenge, such is the domestic strength.

Hanshin regulars get to see quite a few races of significance throughout the year, with the Osaka Hai often used as a springboard by older horses in April, potentially the perfect time to see the beautiful cherry blossom trees around the course. Jump racing is not as big here, which means the well-appointed track in the middle, dotted with meticulously-clipped topiary, is not as busy as it might be.

Kyoto
Japan

LOCATION: IN THE DISTRICT OF FUSHIMI, TEN MILES (16.1KM) SOUTH OF CENTRAL KYOTO

THE TRACK: RIGHT-HANDED, OVAL, TURF OF A LITTLE UNDER A MILE AND A QUARTER (1,894M) WITH FURTHER COURSES INSIDE INCLUDING DIRT OF ONE MILE (1,600M), STEEPLECHASE OF SEVEN FURLONGS (1,400M) AND CHUTES; MEETINGS HELD THROUGHOUT THE YEAR

PRINCIPAL RACES: TENNO SHO (SPRING), APRIL/MAY; KIKUKA SHO (JAPANESE ST LEGER), OCTOBER; MILE CHAMPIONSHIP AND QUEEN ELIZABETH II COMMEMORATIVE CUP, BOTH NOVEMBER

OPENED: 1924

FAMOUS MOMENTS: FIRST WIN FOR BUCHIKO, A FILLY WHOSE COLOURING OF PURE WHITE WITH SPOTS ALL OVER HER COAT GAINED A LARGE FOLLOWING

Watercourses are a major theme of this important racecourse in Western Japan. Kyoto's track sits in the space between the Uji and Katsura rivers, very close to the confluence, and local legend has it that tatami (traditional straw) mats were put into the racecourse's ground to make it less marshy. This is very much a heritage area, famed for its numerous sake breweries, and old wooden boats still make their way down the canals.

The track itself has a lake in the infield and its two large stands, part of a major refurbishment in 1999, are known as Grand Swan and Big Swan after the waterfowl floating on it. There is even a Swan Stakes in the race programme, a prep-race for the Mile Championship at the end of the year.

Along with Tokyo, Kyoto stages many of the country's most significant races. The Tenno Sho (or Emperor's Prize) traces back to 1938, and is such a valuable two-mile (3,200m) prize that it often attracts performers over shorter attempting to stretch out their stamina. No better example came than the brilliant Deep Impact, who smashed a track record which had stood for nine years in the 2006 running. Deep Impact was to lose his record when Kitasan Black went even faster in 2017.

Each November, the Queen Elizabeth II Commemorative Cup, which was opened to international competition in 1999, takes place. In 2010 it was to attract British trainer Ed Dunlop's outstanding globe-trotting mare Snow Fairy, who shot four lengths clear under jockey Ryan Moore. Twelve months later, under an inspired ride from the same jockey, she became the first non-Japanese-trained horse to win the same top-level race back to back.

Kyoto has several features which set it apart from its competitors. It has the only round paddock, with a photogenic gnarled tree in the middle, and it is not completely flat like most of the rest. At the end of the back straight on the turf course is what is known as the 'Yodo Slope', where the gradient rises more than four metres, and places even more of an emphasis on stamina.

Yodo station is directly behind the venue, leading visitors back to the shrines, temples and palaces of a fascinating part of the world.

Picture opposite: *Snow Fairy and jockey Ryan Moore in action at Kyoto*

Tokyo

Japan

LOCATION: IN FUCHU IN GREATER TOKYO, FIFTEEN MILES (24.1KM) WEST OF THE CENTRE OF THE CAPITAL

THE TRACK: LEFT-HANDED, OVAL, TURF COURSE OF JUST OVER A MILE AND A QUARTER (2,083M); WITH DIRT TRACK OF NINE AND A HALF FURLONGS (1,899M) AND STEEPLECHASE OF A LITTLE OVER A MILE (1,675M) ON THE INSIDE; MEETINGS THROUGHOUT THE YEAR

PRINCIPAL RACES: JAPAN CUP, NOVEMBER; TOKYO YUSHUN (JAPANESE DERBY), LATE MAY/EARLY JUNE

OPENED: 1933

FAMOUS MOMENTS: THE 1990 JAPANESE DERBY ATTRACTING RECORD CROWDS OF 196,517

Even knowing Tokyo's main racecourse is actually capable of holding more than 220,000 and has six-tier grandstands, it is still hard to appreciate quite how big it is. Everything is on such a vast scale, from the concourse leading from the station on the main line to Tokyo, to the big screen. After a major renovation in 2007, it was then believed to be the largest arena in the world before being superseded many times over in assorted sporting venues.

The main grandstand is the Fuji View, so called because it offers a glimpse of the snow-capped Japanese landmark on a clear day.

The country's racing was a closed shop for many years, but the development of the Japan Cup as an invitational race in 1981 opened up many new frontiers. It is hugely anticipated, with six-figure attendances. The keenest of fans will actually camp outside overnight and there is little short of a stampede when the gates open on the morning of the race as people run through to reserve their spots in the grandstand. Despite the apparent mayhem due to sheer numbers of people, it is all very well ordered and well behaved.

Racing attracts such a following amongst the Japanese that many will arrive with signs for their favourite horses or jockeys: Yutaka Take, a national hero, and British rider Ryan Moore have had notable fan clubs over the years.

Prize money of hundreds of million yen makes the Japan Cup one of the most valuable races in the world. The overseas challengers have continued to come since the American mare Mairzy Doates triumphed in the inaugural event under jockey Cash Asmussen; Jupiter Island (1986) was a first British winner and further successes for British trainers Sir Michael Stoute (Singspiel 1996, Pilsudski 1997) and Luca Cumani (Alkaased 2005) followed. However, Japanese racing is now so strong that local horses have tended to hold sway, and many European trainers have been put off taking on such stiff competition. Several of the other Group One races have been opened to international contenders, without many takers.

The Yasuda Kinen each June has become a major crowd-puller through popular domestic milers like Vodka and Just A Way, while the Autumn Tenno Sho in October or November provides a valuable target for elite horses en route to the Japan Cup.

Al Rayyan

Qatar

LOCATION: IN THE SUBURB OF AL RAYYAN, SEVEN MILES (11.3KM)
WEST OF CENTRAL DOHA

THE TRACK: RIGHT-HANDED, OVAL; GRASS COURSE OF A MILE AND ONE
FURLONG (1,800M), WITH SAND TRACK INSIDE; MEETINGS HELD FROM
OCTOBER TO MAY, USUALLY ON THURSDAYS

PRINCIPAL RACES: QATAR DERBY, DECEMBER; EMIR'S TROPHY, FEBRUARY

OPENED: 2001

FAMOUS MOMENTS: 2015 EMIR'S TROPHY WINNER DUBDAY BECOMES THE
FIRST QATARI-TRAINED HORSE TO WIN A RACE IN BRITAIN, AT GOODWOOD

They are not afraid to chop and change their plans in Qatar, as evidenced by the myriad of building sites in Doha, a capital city which has been transformed beyond recognition in recent years. It is the same too with racing, which began in organised form in 1975; two more racecourses were constructed during the 1990s, before the venue at Al Rayyan came along. There has been talk of an even glitzier track in the future, with Qatar's officials dreaming of rivalling the festivals of their neighbours in the UAE.

Given that the sport is the hobby of the ruling elite, with the lack of gambling or drinking options tending to deter the expats and holidaymakers, there is no real need to change Al Rayyan. It is not in an obvious place to visit, being in a residential area close to one of the main roads leading out to the desert, but it is very pleasant and well-maintained, planted with trees against a backdrop of white houses and the occasional mosque.

The course is part of a wider complex hosting shows and competitions for other equestrian pursuits. Many of the country's 700 horses are trained at the track, and the circuit is fairly self-contained with programmes of Group races for thoroughbreds and Arabians. Meetings are usually in the evening, when it can be refreshingly cool compared with the heat of the afternoon.

Qatar has been using European racing to promote itself, including sponsorship of the Prix de l'Arc de Triomphe and the Glorious Goodwood festival, and several members of the ruling Al Thani family have considerable interests in the sport. Recently, though, it has been attempting to shine a light on its own attraction with the development of the Emir's Sword Festival. Purses of high six- or even seven-figures for the international races have seen entries made by trainers from as far afield as Britain, America and Japan. Action is interspersed with heats of sprint races, with riders competing in pairs wearing traditional outfits.

This has all happened very rapidly as Qatar's outlook has widened – it was only at the end of 2015 that the Brian Meehan-trained Perkunas became the first European-trained winner in the country, landing the Al Rayyan Stakes ridden by Jamie Spencer.

Riyadh
Saudi Arabia

LOCATION: AT JANADRIYAH, CLOSE TO KING KHALID INTERNATIONAL
AIRPORT, NORTHEAST OF RIYADH
THE TRACK: LEFT-HANDED, OVAL, DIRT COURSE OF A MILE AND A QUARTER
(2,000M); MEETINGS ON FRIDAYS AND SATURDAYS, SEPTEMBER–APRIL
PRINCIPAL RACES: KING ABDULAZIZ CUP, FEBRUARY
OPENED: 2003

There are not too many leisure options under the strict rules of Saudi Arabia, but horseracing is a strange anomaly. While there is certainly no gambling, the sport has long been an interest and play thing of the House of Saud.

An organised Equestrian Club of Riyadh has been in operation since 1965 and this out-of-town King Abdulaziz Racetrack replaced a smaller venue in a residential area in Riyadh. It has a large, floodlit circuit and a 5,000-capacity grandstand, with six floors full of restaurants and private boxes, all designed as a potential international flagship.

Racing is certainly a hobby for the elite here; the majority of runners seem to be owned by the king and his family, and there are few spectators. It is, however, cheap to attend and expats talk of it being a peaceful place to while away a few hours. Most meetings have a mixture of races for Arabian horses and domestically bred and imported thoroughbreds.

King Salman and many of his family have spent plenty of money on horses, including a handful of fruitless attempts at the Dubai World Cup. However, there have been signs that the local horses have some ability, too. It was spelled out loud when Saudi-bred Nashmiah won the 2017 UAE 1000 Guineas in Dubai beating an international field of fillies. Nashmiah's trainer, Frenchman Nicolas Bachalard, is one of several to run private stables for the royal family. 'Racing in Saudi Arabia is racing as a purist, there is no gambling, so they race just to race,' said Bachalard in an interview with *Gulf News*. 'For them, it's about pride and there's a great rivalry and they are working on having better horses to get there.'

Prize money is generous, if not huge, but the King's Cup in February has been won by international jockeys Frankie Dettori and James Doyle in recent times, and always attracts a line-up of jockeys from around the world; even the French maestro-trainer André Fabre has saddled a runner in it.

We might just be hearing more about this course in the future. In early 2018 plans were announced for the King Abdulaziz Horse Championships, an event with, it has been suggested, 'as much as $29m' worth of prizes designed to lure international runners and compete with other major races in the region.

Taif

Saudi Arabia

LOCATION: ON THE EDGE OF TAIF, 107 MILES (172KM) EAST OF THE RED SEA PORT OF JEDDAH

THE TRACK: LEFT-HANDED DIRT CIRCUIT OF A MILE (1,600M); FIXTURES IN JULY AND AUGUST

PRINCIPAL RACES: UM ELQURA UNIVERSAL CUP

When the heat becomes too much to bear at the main circuit in Riyadh, Saudi Arabian racing operations, along with many of the city's residents, decamp almost 500 miles (800km) west to a far more comfortable climate. The King Khalid Racetrack in Taif, lined with trees, is only small, and it does not host top-quality action, and but it has a much-enjoyed festival across the high summer months.

Taif stays cooler due to its elevation, the protection given by the Sarawat Mountains, and its proximity to the Red Sea. It is known for its rosewater, fine fruits and agricultural produce, as well as a spectacular cable-car ride in the mountains.

Whilst there is little to remark about the action on the track, Taif has a notable distinction in the world of racing. It was the birthplace of Prince Khalid Abdullah, successful businessman and member of the House of Saud, who became one of racing's pre-eminent owners and breeders through his Juddmonte Farms operation. Amongst a long list of star-names to have carried his green, pink and white silks was the unbeaten champion-turned-leading stallion Frankel.

Kranji

Singapore

LOCATION: NINE MILES (15KM) NORTHWEST OF THE CENTRE OF
SINGAPORE

THE TRACK: LEFT-HANDED; TURF 'LONG COURSE' ONE AND A QUARTER
MILES (2,000M) WITH 600-YARD (550M) HOME STRAIGHT, 'SHORT
COURSE' ONE AND AN EIGHTH MILES (1,800M) WITH 492-YARD (450M)
HOME STRAIGHT, PLUS CHUTES; SYNTHETIC TRACK JUST UNDER ONE MILE

(1,500M) WITH 437-YARD (400M) HOME STRAIGHT; YEAR-ROUND RACING

PRINCIPAL RACES: SINGAPORE GOLD CUP, NOVEMBER

OPENED: 2000

Organised horseracing has taken place in Singapore since the early nineteenth century, run by the original Singapore Sporting Club – rebranded the Singapore Turf Club in the 1920s – overseen by the Malayan Racing Association. And though an independent jurisdiction now, it retains ties with the three courses in Malaysia: the Turf Clubs at Penang, at Ipoh in Perak state, and at Selangor, close to Kuala Lumpur.

While racing in the neighbouring countries has not always been able to prosper, with the modern racecourse at Kranji as its flagship, Singapore racing has thrived. For more than sixty years, from the days of British colonialism until 1999, regular fixtures took place at Bukit Timah, close to the centre of Singapore. Then, after four years of work, costing many millions of Singapore dollars, the state-of-the-art track was opened in the suburb of Kranji.

Although the racecourse is located some miles from the city centre, the MRT train service, part of one of the most efficient public transport systems in the world, ensures easy access at a reasonable price. The move was hailed a success not just at

home but around the world, especially with the introduction of two international races to showcase what Singapore had to offer. In 2015, these were brought to a halt, with officials saying that they had 'accomplished their objectives', which presumably meant that the profile of the new facility at Kranji had been sufficiently raised. However, an international element to the programme is set to return in 2019.

Kranji has a total of six tracks – a mix of grass and a synthetic surface – to ensure the best conditions for racing and for the 1,250 horses in training at the track. An array of jockeys from around the world competes in the racing, which happens principally on Fridays and Sundays.

Much of the racing is held on the synthetic tracks, but the Singapore Triple Crown, which usually takes place during September, October and November, is on turf. The Raffles Cup, staged over one mile (1,600m), is followed by the Queen Elizabeth II Stakes over one and an eighth miles (1,800m) and the Singapore Gold Cup over one and a quarter miles (2,000m).

Seoul
South Korea

LOCATION: IN THE SUBURB OF GWACHEON, ABOUT TEN MILES (16.1KM) SOUTH OF SEOUL CITY CENTRE
THE TRACK: LEFT-HANDED, OVAL; TWO SAND TRACKS: ONE MILE (1,600M) AND NINE AND A HALF FURLONGS (1,900M); TWO-FURLONG (400M) STRAIGHT; YEAR-ROUND RACING

PRINCIPAL RACES: KOREAN DERBY, MAY; KOREA CUP, SEPTEMBER; GRAND PRIX, DECEMBER
OPENED: 1989
FAMOUS MOMENTS: GRADUAL APPEARANCE OF INTERNATIONAL RUNNERS

Are you feeling happy or are you feeling lucky? Those are the two big options for racegoers attending the programmes that take place at Seoul Race Park – also known as LetsRun Park – on Saturdays and Sundays. The two huge stands that line the final straight are named, respectively, Happyville and Luckyville; Happyville can accommodate 35,000 people and Luckyville 42,000. Usually there are eleven to thirteen races and, in between, gamblers have the added option of betting on races being simulcasted from the Korean Racing Association's tracks at Busan – the country's second largest city – and from the pony racing on Jeju Island.

In 1989 the KRA, the sport's administrator since 1949, moved its principal track from Ttukseom to Gwacheon, where it had developed a facility originally constructed for equestrian events at the previous year's Seoul Olympics. The runners race left-handed on sand tracks, and the track is particularly wide. The stables have capacity for more than 1,400 horses.

In its mission statement, the Association pledges to 'upgrade the Korean horse industry' and that it certainly is achieving. Where once the Grade One feature races were the locally contested nine-furlong (1,800m) Korean Derby in May, the President's Cup over ten furlongs (2,000m) in November and the Korean Grand Prix – eleven and a half furlongs (2,300m) – at the end of the year, Seoul now has international races too. Initially the only links were with Japan and then Singapore, but runners from Hong Kong, Europe and America have subsequently taken up places in the line-up for the Korea Cup over nine furlongs (1,800m) and Korea Sprint over six furlongs (1,200m).

For years, the horses were state-owned, so jockeys wore their own silks to signify who they were, but gradually private owners, some from overseas, have become involved using their own colours. The riders' caps correspond to their places in the stalls.

Though an enhanced place on the horseracing map of the world is not assured, the possibilities for racing in Korea are ever more considerable.

Abu Dhabi
United Arab Emirates

LOCATION: AT THE ABU DHABI EQUESTRIAN CLUB ON THE CITY'S CENTRAL ISLAND

THE TRACK: RIGHT-HANDED, SWEEPING, OVAL; TURF TRACK A MILE AND A QUARTER (2,000M), WITH CHUTES AND TRAINING TRACK INSIDE; MEETINGS HELD FROM NOVEMBER TO MARCH

PRINCIPAL RACES: ABU DHABI CHAMPIONSHIP, MARCH

OPENED: 1980

FAMOUS MOMENTS: BRITISH CHAMPION JOCKEY JIM CROWLEY AND MURAAQIB BEING AWARDED THE WORLD'S MOST VALUABLE PUREBRED ARABIAN RACE, THE SHEIKH ZAYED BIN SULTAN AL NAHYAN JEWEL CROWN, AFTER A STEWARDS' INQUIRY IN 2017

Abu Dhabi's racecourse, close to the Mushrif Palace, which the Emir uses to entertain, spawned from the ruling Al Nahyan family's interest in equestrian culture. It was originally simply a riding club, before races began to be staged behind closed doors between Arabian horses owned by the ruling family. Access to the public began in 1991, followed by an improved surface, state-of-the-art 500-seat grandstand, and air-conditioned stable blocks. The riding school continues, and the facility is also used for international showjumping and long-distance, endurance horse races.

Fixtures, which usually take place under floodlights, are part of the wider UAE circuit, and many of the jockeys who spend time based in nearby Dubai will make the short drive for the midweek fixtures.

Members of the Al Nahyan family, whose investment has provided lucrative prizes for Arabians, have thoroughbred horses trained in France and Britain, as well as a vast private training establishment called Al Asayl some 25 miles (40.2km) out into the desert. Most of the horses racing here are of average ability, but Abu Dhabi provides free entrance and a relaxed atmosphere, and looks likely to continue to grow in line with the city.

Al Ain
United Arab Emirates

LOCATION: AT THE NORTHERN END OF AL AIN, ABU DHABI'S SECOND-BIGGEST CITY, CLOSE TO THE BORDER WITH OMAN

THE TRACK: RIGHT-HANDED, OVAL; SAND TRACK OF JUST OVER ONE AND A HALF MILES (2,500M), WITH SPRINT COURSE AND CHUTES; MEETINGS FROM NOVEMBER TO MARCH

PRINCIPAL RACES: AL AIN MARATHON SERIES

OPENED: 2014

FAMOUS MOMENTS: 5,000 PEOPLE THROUGH THE DOORS FOR THE CURTAIN-RAISER AT THE END OF JANUARY 2014

There was a long wait for racing aficionados of this inland city, an oasis in the desert with thousands of years of history. The Al Ain Equestrian, Shooting and Golf Club track was ten years in the making, and when it was finally opened it became the largest track in the UAE, in terms of race distances if not the venue itself.

While camel racing is a passion of the Emirati population – a far bigger circuit for the hump-backed steeds is just a couple of fields away – it has been the significant Sudanese diaspora who have embraced the horseracing. They flocked to the first fixture to enjoy picnics, and have returned for many more relaxed fixtures, which are of a modest level in terms of quality.

Top international jockeys staying in the UAE tend to drop in, with regular visitor Tadhg O'Shea winning the first-ever race, and leading names Jim Crowley and James Doyle both seen in action. A handful of trainers have taken up residence in the permanent facilities.

There were some teething problems, but this welcoming little track is set to grow.

Jebel Ali
United Arab Emirates

LOCATION: FIFTEEN MILES (24.1KM) DOWN THE COAST FROM THE CITY CENTRE OF DUBAI, CLOSE TO THE MAN-MADE PALM JUMEIRAH ARCHIPELAGO
THE TRACK: RIGHT-HANDED, HORSESHOE-SHAPED DIRT TRACK OF A MILE AND THREE FURLONGS (2,200M); STRAIGHT COURSE OF SEVEN FURLONGS (1,400M); MEETINGS EVERY OTHER FRIDAY, NOVEMBER–MARCH

PRINCIPAL RACES: JEBEL ALI SPRINT, JANUARY; JEBEL ALI MILE, MARCH
OPENED: 1990

While the vast and spectacular construction at Meydan is the modern face of racing in Dubai, in terms of a little more tradition and atmosphere there is no beating Jebel Ali. Small-scale and cosy, it dates back to the beginning of organised thoroughbred racing in Dubai. The track was founded by Sheikh Ahmed Al Maktoum, whose distinctive yellow racing colours were matched on the first grandstand roof; a second head-on facility for members was added in 1993.

The Sheikh employed the expertise of Dhruba Selvaratnam, a Sri Lankan-born trainer, who was serving as an assistant to the great Vincent O'Brien in Ireland at the time he was hired. Together they constructed a course which is unlike any other, with a notably severe, examining uphill finish. The sandy surface, mixed with oil, is deep and demanding, so stamina is a necessity. The course has been given the not-easy-to-acquire endorsement of no less than Lester Piggott. Selvaratnam has remained a trainer at Jebel Ali ever since, saddling numerous winners for Sheikh Ahmed.

With Friday being part of the weekend in Dubai, its casual meetings attract big crowds, while there are usually entertainers and prize giveaways. The racing is usually lower-tier than at Meydan, although good-quality horses have used it for prep races before bigger events at the main track.

The vista has changed markedly since Jebel Ali's opening meeting. The skyscrapers along the seafront loom large beyond the winning post, and the venue itself is now hemmed in by Emirates Hills, a gated community which is home to some of Dubai's most luxurious properties, and other residential areas. The facilities have improved, with seating for 2,000 people and lawns adding to the garden party atmosphere. The infield of the course has been left in its natural state.

Despite being difficult to find – the port of Jebel Ali is further down the coast – and having less ritzy facilities than its neighbours, it has proved popular with a wide range of society, and it does feel pleasantly authentic in a city parts of which are not exactly renowned for that quality.

Given the rapid development of Dubai, one could never be certain that it will remain as it is, but it is to be hoped that officials treasure a hidden gem.

Meydan

United Arab Emirates

LOCATION: EIGHT MILES (12.9KM) SOUTH OF DUBAI CITY

THE TRACK: LEFT-HANDED, OVAL, TURF TRACK OF ONE AND A HALF MILES (2,400M) WITH 492-YARD (450M) HOME STRAIGHT; DIRT TRACK OF ABOUT EIGHT AND THREE-QUARTER FURLONGS (1,750M) WITH 437-YARD (400M) HOME STRAIGHT AND CHUTES; RACING FROM NOVEMBER TO MARCH

PRINCIPAL RACES: DUBAI WORLD CUP, MARCH

OPENED: 2010

FAMOUS MOMENTS: DUBAI WORLD CUP NIGHT IS THE RICHEST RACING FIXTURE IN THE WORLD

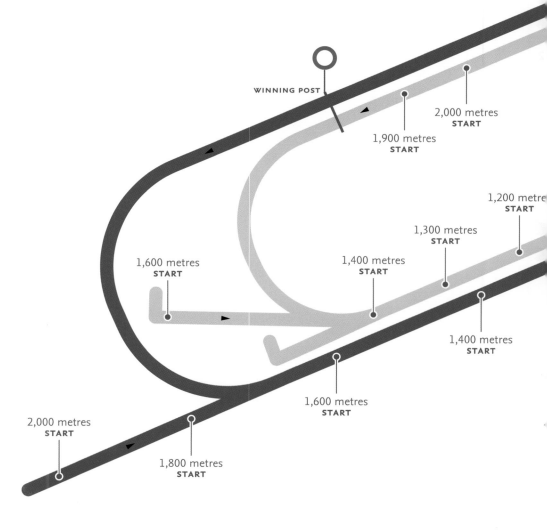

WINNING POST

2,000 metres
START

1,900 metres
START

1,200 metre
START

1,300 metres
START

1,400 metres
START

1,600 metres
START

1,400 metres
START

1,600 metres
START

2,000 metres
START

1,800 metres
START

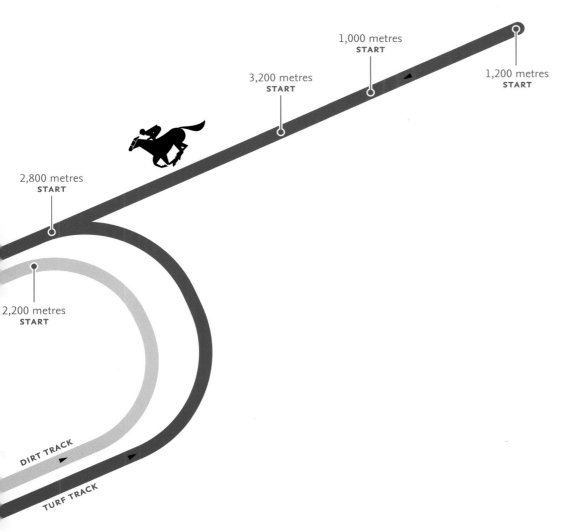

1,200 metres
START

1,000 metres
START

3,200 metres
START

2,800 metres
START

2,200 metres
START

DIRT TRACK

TURF TRACK

The opening of Meydan racecourse in 2010 represented the latest chapter in the colourful horseracing life of Sheikh Mohammed bin Rashid Al Maktoum, the ruler of Dubai. The Sheikh had long demonstrated his passion for all things equestrian, supposedly sharing his breakfast with his horse en route to school. An interest in international racing was heightened by a visit to Newmarket races while studying in the UK during the 1960s, and after his first win as an owner, with Hatta at Brighton in 1977, Sheikh Mohammed and his family went on to create a racehorse-owning and breeding empire around the globe. Most run under his Godolphin banner, named in honour of one of the foundation stallions of the modern thoroughbred.

Meydan, which opened in January 2010 to replace Nad Al Sheba as the number one track, represents a determination to promote Dubai on the world stage by attracting the most outstanding horses on the globe to compete against the best opponents. Indeed 'meydan' translates from the Arabic as 'meeting place'.

To describe the facilities as state-of-the-art seems something of an understatement: the world's largest grandstand boasts a breathtaking crescent roof of energy-efficient solar and titanium panels that can light up the night sky, the total building stretching to as good as one mile in length; capacity is for 60,000 people, with 20,000 of them seated; the car park alone can cope with over 8,500 vehicles. There is also a five-star track-side hotel, all kinds of bars and restaurants, and the stabling, for which no expense was spared, was designed to be second to none.

Situated a short journey away from the bright lights of Dubai City, Meydan has a turf and dirt track. It is on the dirt that the Group One Dubai World Cup is staged on the last Saturday in March. Racing under floodlights, which only adds to the atmosphere of the evening, the runners compete over one and a quarter miles (2,000m), sweeping up in front of the stands before completing a circuit of the course. With its multi-million-dollar purse, the race was the richest international horseracing prize until it was superseded in 2017 by the Pegasus World Cup at Gulfstream Park in Florida.

Sheikh Mohammed inaugurated the Dubai World Cup at Nad Al Sheba in 1996 and, that year, the United States Hall of Fame star Cigar demonstrated he was Flat racing's world champion, winning in a driving finish, ridden by Jerry Bailey. For that first winner to be from America, where owners and trainers have not always been particularly enthusiastic about travelling, was seen as a notable triumph. Since the switch was made to Meydan in 2010, high-profile US challengers California Chrome and Arrogate have shown off their talents by winning.

The World Cup is the final race on a programme of high-grade racing which, combined, offers the richest race-day of the year. The Al Quoz Sprint, the Golden Shaheen, the Dubai Turf and the Sheema Classic are amongst other Group One features on World Cup night. The Sheema Classic, staged over one and a half miles (2,410m), has seen success for major European names like Dar Re Mi, Cirrus Des Aigles, St Nicholas Abbey – owned by Sheikh Mohammed's arch-rival on the world stage, the Irish-based Coolmore operation – Postponed and Jack Hobbs, the latter another big-race winner with the jockey riding in Godolphin's blue silks. Traditionally, the evening ends with a laser show, firework display and a concert by an international star.

The series of high-quality, big money races that make up the Dubai Carnival runs from January to March. Leading racehorse owners, trainers and jockeys fly in and out for the Carnival, which culminates on 'Super Saturday' in early March, something of a dress rehearsal for the big day later in the month.

No betting is allowed in Dubai, though visitors to the track are seen closely studying the form and taking part in 'prediction games', which can yield big dividends.

Horseracing in Dubai – like the state itself – has come a very long way in a very short time, and Sheikh Mohammed is renowned for always striving to move forward. With that in mind: whatever next?

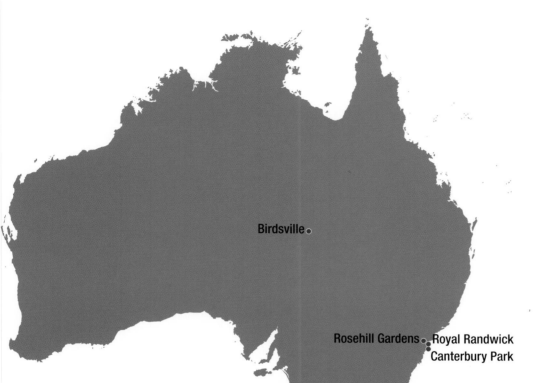

Birdsville

Rosehill Gardens • Royal Randwick
Canterbury Park

Dunkeld •
Flemington • Moonee Valley
Caulfield

Ellerslie •

Otaki •

Trentham •

Oceania

Birdsville

Australia

LOCATION: 982 MILES (1,580KM) WEST OF BRISBANE, QUEENSLAND

THE TRACK: LEFT-HANDED, ALMOST SQUARE, CLAYPAN TRACK
SURROUNDED BY SAND DUNES, CIRCUIT OF ONE AND A QUARTER MILES
(2,000M); FIXTURE IN SEPTEMBER

PRINCIPAL RACES: BIRDSVILLE CUP, SEPTEMBER

OPENED: 1882

FAMOUS MOMENTS: WEATHERING A SANDSTORM

The remarkable track at Birdsville has become something of a bucket list essential for any racing fan in Australia, despite its famously remote location. The tiny outback town, with barely more than one hundred inhabitants, was where farmers paid tolls when moving stock over the state border between Queensland and South Australia. The racecourse was set up in 1882 and has changed little since, though races are no longer started by the drop of a hat.

Coming by land and air, racegoers swell the population to 7,000-plus during the two-day September carnival, the sole fixture of the year. Those that choose to drive have the option of taking in the events set up along the way, including the annual Yabby (crayfish) race in Windorah.

Birdsville's caravan park and its hotel are permanently booked up for carnival week, so visiting fans lodge in 'Tent City', a temporary rest area allocated to racegoers. The evening party and social events are so notoriously raucous that even on the rare occasions that the racing has been cancelled (2007 and 2010), and racegoers marooned, the social events still went on.

Canterbury Park

Australia

LOCATION: IN THE RIVERSIDE SUBURB OF CANTERBURY, EIGHT MILES (12.9KM) SOUTHWEST OF CENTRAL SYDNEY

THE TRACK: RIGHT-HANDED, PEAR-SHAPED CIRCUIT OF ABOUT A MILE (1,579M), WITH 350-YARD (320M) HOME STRAIGHT AND SEVERAL CHUTES FOR SHORTER RACES; RACING THROUGHOUT THE YEAR, USUALLY ON MIDWEEK EVENINGS

PRINCIPAL RACES: CANTERBURY CLASSIC, JANUARY

OPENED: 1871

FAMOUS MOMENTS: KINGSTON TOWN, ONE OF AUSTRALIA'S GREATEST HORSES, FINISHING LAST IN A HIGHLY INAUSPICIOUS RACECOURSE DEBUT IN MARCH 1979

Close to the heart of Sydney and facing the Cooks River, Canterbury seems to have fallen down the region's racing pecking order, which is a great pity. It allows spectators to be up close to the action, with its well-draining track generally providing fairly run races as jockeys know that it will be hard to make up ground on the short home straight.

In its early days it shared space with a lovingly maintained garden – looked after by one George Monk, a renowned cultivator of pansies – which included a zoo featuring kangaroos and emus. The space was requisitioned during the Second World War, though racing continued throughout, and a team of American fighter planes even flew over during a meeting in 1942, perhaps to remind Australians of their presence to defend the country against possible attack.

There are many Sydneysiders who have fond memories of the place, but what was once a strong racing programme has been somewhat neglected, and Canterbury no longer stages any hugely significant races. In the past it was home to the Canterbury Stakes, a Group One sprint won by the phenomenal Manikato in 1982, but the Sydney racing authorities moved that race to Rosehill and then Randwick to boost the premier venues. The Canterbury Guineas was also lost to Randwick after Octagonal took it en route to an Australian Triple Crown in 1996.

So You Think, who took Europe by storm and won the 2012 Prince of Wales's Stakes at Royal Ascot on transfer to trainer Aidan O'Brien in Ireland, was perhaps the last top-notcher to set foot at Canterbury, warming up in a barrier trial before embarking upon his public racing career.

Emphasis nowadays is on the entertainment side of the sport and Canterbury began to host the city's first evening meetings at the turn of the century. Under floodlights, much in the mould of Moonee Valley in Melbourne, they have mushroomed as attempts are made to lure metropolitan society. Often with free entry and next to a railway station, it ought to work.

Unfortunately, its prime location in a thriving city leads to concerns about Canterbury's future. It was originally owned or leased from private landowners, but belongs to the Australian Turf Club these days, though property developers have been sniffing around the 86-acre site ever more loudly.

Caulfield

Australia

LOCATION: SEVEN MILES (11.3KM) SOUTHEAST OF CENTRAL MELBOURNE

THE TRACK: LEFT-HANDED, TRIANGULAR-SHAPED, TURF CIRCUIT OF JUST OVER A MILE AND A QUARTER (2,080M), WITH CHUTES, 401-YARD (367M) HOME STRAIGHT, SAND AND GRASS TRAINING TRACKS INSIDE; MEETINGS THROUGHOUT THE YEAR

PRINCIPAL RACES: CAULFIELD CUP, OCTOBER

OPENED: 1859

FAMOUS MOMENTS: THE WORST SET OF FALLS IN AUSTRALIA'S HISTORY, WITH FIFTEEN HORSES COMING DOWN IN THE 1885 CAULFIELD CUP, CONTRIBUTING TO THE DEATH OF JOCKEY DONALD NICOLSON

Still affectionately known as 'The Heath', early Caulfield was countryside where riders would compete through hills and snake-infested scrubland. Investment from the Victorian Amateur Turf Club saw a formalised track fashioned by 1876, and nowadays, surrounded by the Melbourne suburbs and with its immaculate glass-fronted grandstand, it is a modern wonder staging some of the city's best racing.

As much as the Melbourne Cup would be named by most as Australia's most famous race, the Caulfield Cup would not be considered too far behind it in national terms. Held only a few weeks before the Flemington race, despite its own status it

can be overshadowed and become something of a prep for its illustrious cousin, albeit over a shorter distance. Nonetheless it is still very valuable, and it has proved fiendishly difficult to achieve the double, with just nine horses managing the feat between Poseidon in 1906 and Ethereal in 2001.

The Caulfield Cup is part of a carnival meeting during mid-October and early November, which dominates the Melbourne sporting agenda, attracting between 30,000 and 50,000 people. Attendance was even larger in times gone by, notably when Bernborough appeared in the 1946 race in front of what was believed to be a crowd of more than 108,000. The horse had accrued a fifteen-race winning streak, earning comparisons with the legendary Phar Lap.

Bernborough was considered a certainty, and a mysterious, elegantly dressed gambler from Sydney, Johanna Taks, famously staked a simply colossal £6,500 – some said much more – in bets

on him, only to lose the lot when the horse managed just fifth place under a welterweight of 10st 10lb. There were allegations that he had been 'got at', and jockey Athol 'George' Mulley was sacked and never spoke to trainer Harry Plant again. Taks told reporters that she had been confident with her gigantic bet because Bernborough 'had looked so lovely before the race'.

Mystery also surrounded the 1922 renewal when a suspicious fire broke out on the eve of the race, burning down the members' grandstand, weighing room and a number of other buildings. It was thought to be an act of revenge by underworld figure 'Squizzy' Taylor, although this was never proved. Extraordinarily, the race still went ahead the next day.

The Cup has been open to international competition since 1998, when Taufan's Melody scored a famous win for British trainer Lady Herries, before finishing fourth in the Melbourne Cup a few weeks later.

Dunkeld

Australia

LOCATION: IN THE TOWN OF DUNKELD (POPULATION 700), 160 MILES (257.5KM) WEST OF MELBOURNE
THE TRACK: LEFT-HANDED, OVAL, TURF OF ONE MILE (1,600M), 219-YARD (200M) HOME STRAIGHT; ONE MEETING A YEAR ON A SATURDAY, MID-NOVEMBER
PRINCIPAL RACES: DUNKELD CUP

OPENED: 1948
FAMOUS MOMENTS: ORGANISERS TOAST A MODERN-DAY RECORD CROWD OF 10,000 AT THE 2017 MEETING

Australia has a strong affinity for its rural racecourses, where the usually temporary facilities bring communities together once or twice a year for their own Cup day.

Dunkeld is one of the country's best known thanks to its spectacular scenery. The sharp oval is guarded by the jagged slopes of Mount Abrupt, at the southern tip of the Grampians National Park. Punters have been coming together for racing in this area since before the formation of the Dunkeld Race Club in 1948, and the event has grown notably in recent times, with best-dressed competitions and marquees lining the course as far as the home turn.

Racing in Victoria is hierarchical, and most of the trainers from the Melbourne area would be unlikely to take horses to the country circuit, so, with its generally low prize money and most races being for low-grade maidens and handicappers, it is left to the amateurs and provincial handlers. For many visitors, however, just being somewhere so beautiful in the Australian spring makes the quality of the racing of little consequence.

Flemington

Australia

LOCATION: IN THE MELBOURNE SUBURB OF FLEMINGTON, ABOUT THREE AND A HALF MILES NORTHWEST OF THE CITY CENTRE

THE TRACK: LEFT-HANDED, PEAR-SHAPED, TURF, JUST UNDER ONE AND A HALF MILES (2,312M) WITH CHUTES, 492-YARD (450M) HOME STRAIGHT; RACES STAGED YEAR-ROUND EXCEPT DECEMBER

PRINCIPAL RACES: MELBOURNE CUP, 3PM, FIRST TUESDAY IN NOVEMBER

OPENED: 1840

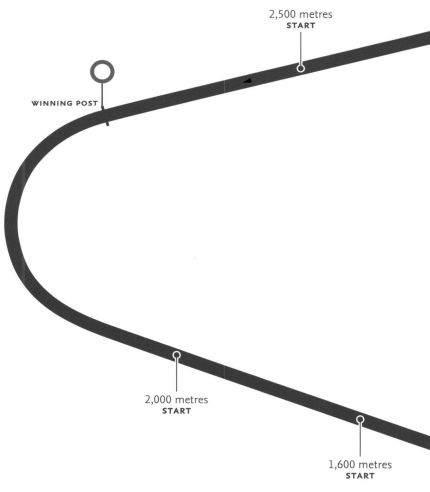

2,500 metres
START

WINNING POST

2,000 metres
START

1,600 metres
START

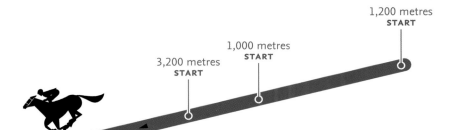

1,200 metres
START

1,000 metres
START

3,200 metres
START

1,400 metres
START

Sport is an integral part of Australia's culture, and Melbourne, the state capital of Victoria, epitomises that feature as one of the greatest sporting cities in the world. Aussie Rules Football and premier cricket matches are held at the Melbourne Cricket Ground all year round, while just over the train tracks tennis' first Grand Slam of the year is played. However, it is horseracing that takes centre stage in the city during the spring (October and November) and Flemington, the headquarters of Australian racing, is at its centre.

The first race meeting was held only five years after the founding of Melbourne, on a site that became known as Flemington after the Scottish home of the property owner's wife. Today there is racing held most of the year – all of it on the flat after jump racing ceased in 2008 – with the Melbourne Cup, the world's premier long-distance handicap, in November.

Inaugurated in 1861, the Melbourne Cup is staged over two miles (3,200m) and has gained the world-famous reputation as 'the race that stops a nation'. 4,000 people saw Archer win the first running, before he followed up a year later. As early as the 1880s, six-figure crowds were seen for Melbourne Cup day, at a time when the city's population was merely 290,000. It was the most fashionable event of the year. In 1875, 'Cup day' was made a public holiday, further cementing horseracing's place in the fabric of Australian culture.

The champion New Zealand-bred racehorse Phar Lap – the chestnut dubbed the 'Red Terror' and 'Big Red' for his victories in thirty-seven races – was one of the race's great winners, in 1930. He was later moved to the United States by his American owner, winning the hugely valuable Agua Caliente Handicap in Mexico in a record-breaking time. However, his fame – and success – was ultimately his downfall. Having survived being shot at from a parked car whilst returning from exercise before the Melbourne Cup, he died in April 1932 as a result of arsenic poisoning. To this day, theories swirl as to whether the poisoning was a deliberate act or not; many believe American gangsters killed the horse because his dominance could cripple their underground gambling activities, though others believe it is more likely that he accidentally consumed weedkiller.

Phar Lap's significance endures: his mounted hide is displayed in the Melbourne Museum; his skeleton in New Zealand's Te Papa Tongarewa museum in Wellington; and his (notably large) heart in the National Museum of Australia in Canberra. He also features in the Australian citizenship test.

In a country famed for its propensity for great fillies and mares, including Black Caviar, Sunline and Winx, another female horse – Makybe Diva – hit centre stage at Flemington in 2005, when taking the Melbourne Cup for a record third time. In all, she won fifteen races and over A$14 million in prize money. Owned by fisherman Tony Šantić, and named by taking the first two letters of his employees' names (Maureen, Kylie, Belinda, Diane and Vanessa), her wins in 2003 and 2004 led to the allocation of a vast weight in 2005, yet that was still not enough to stop the sequence. Commentator Greg Miles was able to utter the immortal words 'a champion becomes a legend' as she passed the line in front on what was to be her final race start.

In 2015 the Melbourne Cup again made world headlines when Michelle Payne became the first woman to ride the winner of the race, aboard outsider Prince Of Penzance. Straight afterwards, she spoke up passionately for her sex in racing by telling detractors to 'get stuffed, because women can do anything and we can beat the world'.

The race received considerable international interest after Irish trainer Dermot Weld blazed the trail for the Europeans by winning Cups with Vintage Crop (1993) and Media Puzzle (2002). It is now a key target for overseas horses, with runners from Germany, France, Japan and Ireland again winning in the early years of the twenty-first century.

Amongst the foreign challengers, a huge favourite with the Australian crowds was British-trained Red Cadeaux, who finished runner-up in three of his five tries. He was injured on his final attempt in 2015, later dying following complications to his fetlock surgery, and was buried at Flemington. A Pom maybe, but a Cup legend for Aussies.

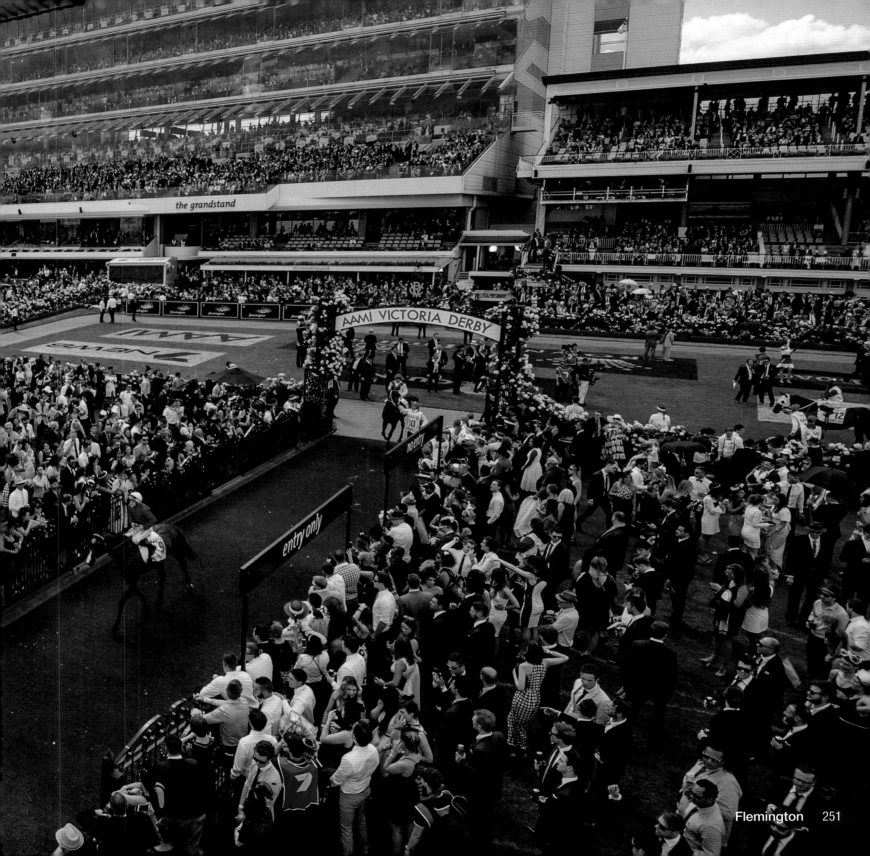

the grandstand

the mounting yard

AAMI VICTORIA DERBY

no entry

entry only

Moonee Valley
Australia

LOCATION: NINE MILES (14.5KM) NORTH OF CENTRAL MELBOURNE

THE TRACK: LEFT-HANDED, SQUARE-SHAPED TRACK OF A MILE AND ONE FURLONG (1,800M) WITH 186-YARD (170M) HOME STRAIGHT; MEETINGS THROUGHOUT THE YEAR, LARGELY ON FRIDAY EVENINGS

PRINCIPAL RACES: THE COX PLATE, OCTOBER

OPENED: 1883

FAMOUS MOMENTS: 'THE VALLEY IS ROCKING AND THE WORLD IS KNOCKING' – THE COMMENTATOR AS WINX EQUALS RECORD FOR COX PLATE WINS IN 2017

In much the same way that no one would design a racecourse around the cambers of Epsom Downs in the modern age, it is hard to imagine a new track being constructed in the mould of Moonee Valley. There is not a contemporary track in the world with as short a run-in as this one, tucked away just off one of the main arterial roads leading out through the north of Melbourne.

The Valley itself is one of the great institutions of this sports-mad city, as it holds the country's biggest weight-for-age race, the Cox Plate. The one-and-a-quarter-mile (2,040m) championship event, held during the Australian spring, is named after William Samuel Cox, who leased this tranche of what was then farmland in 1882 and began staging race meetings there from a year later. Its first race resulted in a dead heat and there have been close finishes ever since; with such a short run home, many will be in with a chance on the dash for a line.

Cox himself spawned a racing dynasty, with members of the family holding positions of high office at the track for almost another century. One of his sons, W.S. Cox Jr, was an accomplished jump jockey and completed an unprecedented 1892 double aboard

Redleap when winning both the Grand National Hurdle in July and Grand National Steeplechase a month later with a huge weight on his back.

Moonee Valley remains under the private ownership of its racing club, unlike most other important Australian racecourses, so is able to make its own decisions. The club has pioneered popular Friday evening meetings under the floodlights and built up a formidable programme. The Cox Plate is its chief asset, and its previous winners are something of a 'Who's Who' of Australian racing, with great names like Phar Lap, Kingston Town, Makybe Diva, Sunline and the phenomenal Winx all on the roll of honour. There has been an attempt to attract overseas runners with increasing prize money.

Grand plans involving some residential development are in the pipeline, which would mean some realigning of the track and lengthening of the run-in. Whilst this change might lose a tiny bit of Moonee Valley's unique characteristic, it at least should safeguard its future.

Rosehill Gardens

Australia

LOCATION: IN THE SUBURB OF PARRAMATTA, SIXTEEN MILES (25.7KM) WEST OF CENTRAL SYDNEY

THE TRACK: RIGHT-HANDED, ALMOST SQUARE, TURF CIRCUIT OF ONE AND A QUARTER MILES (2,048M) WITH A HOME STRAIGHT OF A QUARTER OF A MILE (408M); SECOND TURF TRACK INSIDE; FIXTURES HELD THROUGHOUT THE YEAR

PRINCIPAL RACES: GOLDEN SLIPPER, APRIL

OPENED: 1885

FAMOUS MOMENTS: IRISH-TRAINED GLOBETROTTER GORDON LORD BYRON CAUSES BIG-ODDS SHOCK AFTER ACCEPTING AN INVITATION TO THE 2014 GEORGE RYDER STAKES AS A RARE OVERSEAS CHALLENGER

With a name like Rosehill Gardens, one might imagine this grand old racecourse has some long-standing relationship with the floral blooms which abound in it. In fact, the land on which the commuter town of Parramatta is located was cleared by the early founder of Sydney, Arthur Philip, and named Rose Hill after his friend, the British politician George Rose.

The track itself was founded by John Bennett, a theatre impresario, who bought the land, and completed building work by 1885, for an estimated £12,000. For good measure, he even constructed a branch line and railway station so people could get there. Folk were impressed. 'Of the Rosehill racecourse too much can hardly be said,' raved *The Freeman's Journal*. 'The course is one of the best appointed and neatest that can be found in any part of the colonies.' Although the growth of Sydney means that Rosehill is no longer in the countryside, it has retained its tree-lined nature and its gardens are one of its biggest selling points.

While Victoria dominates the Australian spring, the most important time of year for New South Wales racing is in the autumn. During weekends in March and April some huge prizes are raced for at Rosehill and Randwick, bringing with them the stylishly dressed crowds, regardless of the unpredictable weather.

This place's most famous trophy is the Golden Slipper, worth A$3.5 million and the world's richest two-year-old race. Suffice to say it attracts the speediest of youngsters, who will guarantee themselves a place at stud with a victory at such a young age.

The George Ryder, originally known as the Railway Stakes, has been a Group One since 1980 and, over an extended seven furlongs (1,400m), attracts versatile Australian stars such as Winx, Manikato and Lohnro. Chris Waller, the New Zealand-born trainer of Winx, has his main base at the course. Meanwhile the BMW, a weight-for-age mile-and-a-half (2,400m) race, is often a target for Melbourne Cup-types including three-time Cup winner Makybe Diva.

City rivalry with Melbourne is intense and authorities have also boosted their own spring programme, with Rosehill hosting plenty of valuable prizes through August and September. They aspire for it to become one of the world's premier venues, with a modernisation of the grandstand and facilities in 2015. Even more ambitious projects for hotels and leisure complexes have been mooted for the future.

Royal Randwick
Australia

LOCATION: SIX MILES (9.7KM) SOUTHEAST OF CENTRAL SYDNEY

THE TRACK: ALMOST RECTANGULAR TURF TRACK, A MILE AND THREE FURLONGS (2,224M) IN CIRCUMFERENCE WITH A HOME STRAIGHT OF 448 YARDS (410M)

PRINCIPAL RACES: THE EVEREST

OPENED: 1833 (CLOSED IN 1838 AND REOPENED 1860)

FAMOUS MOMENTS: BLACK CAVIAR GAINS HER TWENTY-FIFTH CONSECUTIVE WIN RACING AT RANDWICK, 2013; THAT RECORD BEING EQUALLED BY WINX AT THE TRACK, 2018

While tourists in Sydney flock to the Opera House or Harbour Bridge, visitors with an appetite for all things equine make sure to find their way to Royal Randwick.

In 1833, Governor Richard Bourke designated the Randwick area for racecourse use, and racing commenced later that year. It was originally called the 'Sandy Course' because of the nature of the ground, and the first race held was between just two horses. However, while the course successfully held meetings up until 1838, what seems to have been a growing unpopularity amongst

Sydney's elite led to its closure, and use for training purposes only. Reinvigorated by the Australian Jockey Club under the presidency of Sir Edward Deas Thomson, a new timber grandstand was constructed, and racing returned to the track in May 1860 in front of 6,000 racegoers.

Royal Randwick has been visited twice by Queen Elizabeth II, in 1954 and 1992, and a year after her 1954 visit, the course renamed the long-running prestigious AJC Plate the Queen Elizabeth Stakes; it is now the richest prize in the Sydney Autumn Carnival. In 1992, when opening the new Paddock Stand, the Queen granted permission for the course to add 'Royal' to its official title.

Legends of Australian racing are inducted into the Australian Hall of Fame, and rarely has an honour been as well-received as it was for trainer Tommy 'TJ' Smith, who secured every Sydney trainers' championship between 1953 and 1985, with over one hundred Group One victories at Randwick. During his lengthy time at the top, Smith trained revered stars including the incredibly versatile Tulloch, who won over both five furlongs (1,000m) and two miles (3,200m) during his outstanding racing career, and Kingston Town, the first horse ever to win three Cox Plates.

Randwick posthumously honoured the trainer in 1999 by renaming the autumn six-furlong (1,200m) sprint the TJ Smith Stakes. Given Group One status in 2005, two of Australia's Royal Ascot winners have since won the prestigious race: Black Caviar and rags-to-riches gelding, Takeover Target.

In 2017, as a challenge to the Melbourne Cup's hegemony of Australian racing, the Australian Turf Club announced the A$10 million sprint prize The Everest. It is now the richest prize conducted on turf in the world and its inaugural running was won by Redzel.

Ellerslie
New Zealand

LOCATION: FOUR AND A HALF MILES (7.2KM) FROM THE CENTRE OF AUCKLAND

THE TRACK: RIGHT-HANDED, OVAL WITH CHUTES, TURF FOR FLAT AND JUMP RACING, CIRCUIT OF JUST OVER A MILE AND ONE FURLONG (1,845M)

PRINCIPAL RACES: AUCKLAND CUP, MARCH

OPENED: 1874

FAMOUS MOMENTS: FIRST FULLY-MECHANISED TOTALISATOR OPERATED, 1913

Ellerslie racecourse in Auckland, on New Zealand's North Island, is the country's premier racecourse, and holds a significant place in the history of betting.

From the mid-nineteenth century the pari-mutuel, a totalisator system pioneered in France, operated around the world. Bets staked on each horse were added up, a commission deducted, and a dividend declared, dependent on how much was in the pool. However, there were problems, not least because those placing their bets did not know how much they would get back on their fancy, and the machinery in use was labour-intensive, unwieldy and sometimes unreliable (bets were lost). But in 1909 inventor George Julius came up with a completely mechanised totalisator which could deal with up to thirty horses being backed simultaneously. At the Easter fixture at Ellerslie in 1913, Julius' system was employed for the first time, working efficiently and giving everyone the chance to see likely dividends as the bets rolled in. The system was manufactured for years afterwards.

Racing started in Auckland in 1842 at a place known as Epsom Downs. Originally, there was a Jockey Club and a Turf Club, who fell out over which one was the more important, and members ended up amalgamating as the Auckland Racing Club. The racecourse was developed on land purchased from a Scottish-born entrepreneur named Robert Graham, who owned a zoo and exquisitely manicured gardens, a legacy that lives on in the grounds at the track.

1874 saw the first races, including the initial staging of the prize that remains the annual feature, the Grade One Auckland Cup over two miles (3,200m). Since 2007, after a move from Christmas, the race has been positioned in March as the centrepiece of Auckland Cup week. The Grade One New Zealand Derby also takes place in March, while the Karaka Million races are the highlight of January. Ellerslie's jump racing calendar includes the gruelling four-mile (6,400m) Great Northern Steeplechase in September.

Horses trained and bred in New Zealand have made a notable impact in Australia. The legendary Phar Lap is one, while the mare Sunline won the Cox Plate at Moonee Valley twice and was Australian Horse of the Year three times. Considered a great of Kiwi sport, she is buried at Ellerslie.

Otaki

New Zealand

LOCATION: IN THE TINY COASTAL TOWN OF OTAKI (POPULATION 6,000), AROUND FORTY-FIVE MILES (72.4KM) NORTHEAST OF WELLINGTON

THE TRACK: LEFT-HANDED, OVAL, TURF OF ABOUT MILE AND ONE FURLONG (1,800M); MEETINGS HELD THROUGHOUT THE YEAR

PRINCIPAL RACES: OTAKI-MAORI WFA CLASSIC, FEBRUARY

OPENED: 1910

FAMOUS MOMENTS: A TROPHY, PRESENTED FOR A RACE AT THE OTAKI MAORI RACING CLUB'S NEW YEAR MEETING AT RIKIRIKI IN 1892 BUT THEN LOST IN A STOREROOM FOR 120 YEARS, BEING REPAIRED AND AWARDED AGAIN FOR THE ST LEGER TRIAL IN 2012

To give it its full title, The Otaki-Maori Racing Club (OMRC) is the only institution of its type in the world. The indigenous people of New Zealand developed an affinity with horses when they were introduced to the country in the early nineteenth century and races were soon being staged. This racing club is the only one remaining, and while 'Europeans' are allowed to be members of sorts, only those descended from the Ngāti Raukawa, Ngāti Toa and Te Āti Awa tribes can become officials and committee members.

This is not to say the racecourse is an all-Maori concern; the Otaki racecourse is on the national programme and everyone is welcome to come and enjoy a relaxed day's racing in the countryside. The action has generally been of a mid-level, although its first stakes race, the WFA Classic, was introduced in 1986 as the fourth richest sprint in the country at the time. It was won by 25-1 chance Peat. Now a Group One race each February, it was won in 2006 by Michael Walker, a jockey of Maori descent who has gone on to be one of the leading riders in Australia.

The OMRC itself, formed in 1886, pre-dates the venue, which came about after lease problems with the former track at Rikiriki. There used to be steeplechase races but there were problems with the racing surface, owing to the proximity of the river. A motor race, rather unfortunately staged in 1927, probably did not help the matter. Vast remedial work in 1960 rectified the problem, but the club neglected to upgrade the facilities at the same time, and when, in the early 1970s, the New Zealand authorities were considering centralising racing, the course was threatened with closure, as it was considered sub-standard compared with nearby Levin. A public outcry stopped this, and construction of two new stands took place in the next couple of decades.

The racecourse hosts several days of trotting and has stepped in to hold a few days on behalf of the Levin Racing Club, whose nearby track was shut to become a training centre in 1990. The Levin Classic, another Group One race, was held at Otaki for a decade before being moved to the Trentham track nearer Wellington. The Interislander Summer Festival fixture each January is another vibrant and enjoyable occasion in the calendar.

Trentham
New Zealand

LOCATION: ON THE WESTERN SIDE OF THE CITY OF UPPER HUTT, TWENTY-ONE MILES (33.8KM) NORTHEAST OF WELLINGTON

THE TRACK: LEFT-HANDED, IRREGULAR OVAL, TURF COURSE OF A MILE AND A QUARTER (2,000M) WITH 492-YARD (450M) HOME STRAIGHT; FIGURE-OF-EIGHT STEEPLECHASE COURSE ON THE INFIELD; MEETINGS BETWEEN OCTOBER AND JUNE

PRINCIPAL RACES: WELLINGTON CUP, JANUARY; NEW ZEALAND OAKS, MARCH

OPENED: 1906

FAMOUS MOMENTS: NEW ZEALAND-BRED RACEHORSE ICON PHAR LAP STAYS AT TRENTHAM PRIOR TO HIS CONTROVERSIAL TRANSFER TO AMERICA, ATTRACTING HUGE CROWDS JUST TO WATCH HIM EXERCISE

Although regarded as Wellington's racecourse, and easily accessible to the New Zealand capital, a very rural setting greets visitors to Trentham as they look out onto the tree-covered mountain slopes. This venerable racecourse, used as a military hospital and a home for American troops during the Second World War, has maintained a number of its old facilities.

Trentham stages plenty of important racing annually but the showcase time of year is in January, with big fixtures taking place on three consecutive Saturdays, and crowds encouraged to dress up. Pride of place goes to the Wellington Cup which, although downgraded to a Group Three race, is one of New Zealand's most famous honours and a stayers' championship. It pre-dates Trentham, having been first held at the now defunct Hutt Park from 1874. Organisers initially went to the extent of importing extravagant silver trophies from Mappin & Webb jewellers in Britain, and the 1894 Cup is still in the possession of the Wellington Racing Club. Manufacture of the new trophy – issued each year – was transferred to New Zealand early in the last century; the design changes constantly, but they are still hand-made and greatly coveted by the leading owners.

The Flat is certainly the best-known branch of racing at Trentham and indeed across New Zealand, but there is a distinct jumping heritage here too. Seagram, winner of the 1991 Grand National at Aintree, was bred by Jeanette Broome and was one of a number of Kiwi horses imported to the UK by the late trainer David Barons.

While there are only around 100 races during the winter, Trentham boasts a couple of its better-quality prizes, the Wellington Hurdle and Wellington Steeplechase, on the same card in July. Each is worth about NZ$75,000.

The hurdle races are simply races over portable obstacles around the Flat course, but the chase course is rather more special. It is not marked out by rails, yet the runners snake in a figure-of-eight over the live-hedge fences and around cricketing nets and rugby pitches. A red-jacketed huntsman marshals the proceedings, adding to the timeless feel of a spectacle which is supposedly best enjoyed from the top of the old Public Stand, a construction completed in 1924.

Glossary

All-weather – a catch-all expression to describe synthetic racing surfaces.

Arabian horse – ancient breed originating in Arabia, ancestors of the thoroughbred.

Arc – Prix de l'Arc de Triomphe, ParisLongchamp, October.

Breeders' Cup – the 'World Championship' of horseracing staged every autumn (fall) since 1984 at a racecourse in North America.

Carnival – alternative to racing 'festival' particularly in Australia.

Cheltenham – British jump racing's principal festival staged every March.

Classic – five premier races mainly for the 3-year-old, 'Classic generation', with origins in the UK but copied worldwide; names and distances can vary, but traditionally the 2000 and the fillies-only 1000 Guineas are staged over a mile, followed by the Oaks (fillies only) and Derby at one-mile and a half and the St Leger over one and three-quarters of a mile.

Colt – male horse.

Dirt – a non-turf racing surface used principally in North America.

Filly – female horse.

Furlong – racing's historic measuring unit, 1/8th of a mile, just over 200 metres.

Gelding – castrated horse.

Group One, Group Two, Group Three, Listed – the top four levels of Flat racing; Group is replaced by Grade in some jurisdictions.

Guinea – £1.05p, the unit of prize money for the original stagings of the 2000 Guineas and 1000 Guineas, and still used at many British horse sales.

Hippodrome (French), Hipódromo (Spanish/Portugese) – racecourse.

Jockey Club – the original regulator of British racing, emulated around the world, in some jurisdictions known as the Turf Club.

Match – race for two horses.

Meet – fixture, or series of fixtures, particularly in the US.

National Hunt – jump racing.

PMU – Pari Mutuel Urbain; all stakes are placed in a 'pool' which is then divided up to calculate dividends; also known as a totalisator or tote.

Quarter horse – American-bred horses, very fast over short distances.

Seabiscuit – American racing great of the 1930s.

Secretariat – American racing great of the 1970s.

Sport of Kings – historic nickname given to horseracing because of Royal connections.

Stud book – register of thoroughbreds.

Thoroughbred – the type of horse mainly employed for horseracing.

Trotting or harness racing – 'standardbred' horses pulling a 'sulky' (cart) at trotting speed.

Triple Crown – a hat-trick of success in the 2000 or 1000 Guineas, the Oaks or Derby and the St Leger, or their equivalents.

US Triple Crown – the Kentucky Derby, Preakness Stakes and Belmont Stakes.

Index

Image Credits

Front cover: © Healy Racing
Back cover: © Michael Dodge/Getty Images
Endpaper front: © Frank Sorge
Endpaper back: © Frank Sorge
Contents page: © Ichiro Terashima
Foreword: © Alan Crowhurst/Getty Images
Introduction: © Dan Abraham-focusonracing.com
Ostend: © Georges Jansoone - This file is licensed under the Creative Commons Attribution-Share Alike 3.0 Unported license.
Pardubice: © Frank Sorge
Auteil: © Frank Sorge/galoppfoto.de/Brose
Chantilly: © Frank Sorge
Deauville-La Touques: © Frank Sorge / © focusonracing.com
ParisLongchamp: © Dan Abraham - focusonracing.com
Hoppegarten: © Frank Sorge
Baden-Baden: © Frank Sorge/galoppfoto.de/Bander
Kincsem Park: © Frank Sorge/Galoppfoto
Curragh: © Healy Racing
Laytown: © Healy Racing
Leopardstown: © FrankSorge / © Healy Racing
Punchestown: © Healy Racing
Fairyhouse: © Healy Racing
Capannelle: © Debbie Burt
Duindigt: © Peter Horree / Alamy Stock Photo
Służewiec: © Equine Creative Media
Moscow: © Frank Sorge
Bro Park: © Steven Cargill / Racingfotos.com
Jägersro: © Frank Sorge/galoppfoto.de/Ploff
St Moritz: © Frank Sorge
Veliefendi: © Liesl King
Aintree: © Dan Abraham - focusonracing.com / © Dan Abraham - focusonracing.com/Public Domain
Ascot: © Dan Abraham - focusonracing.com
Cheltenham: © Dan Abraham-focusonracing.com / © Healy Racing-focusonracing.com
Chester: © Dan Abraham-focusonracing.com
Doncaster: © Dan Abraham-focusonracing.com
Epsom: © Dan Abraham-focusonracing.com
Goodwood: © Dan Abraham / © Dan Abraham-focusonracing.com
Newmarket: © Dan Abraham-focusonracing.com / © Dan Abraham - racingfotos.com
York: © Dan Abraham - focusonracing.com
Garrison Savannah: © dupratphotos
Hastings Park: © Liang Sen/Xinhua / Alamy Stock Photo
Martinique: © Forget Patrick / Alamy Stock Photo
Mexico City: © dupratphotos
Panama City: © dupratphotos
Arlington: © dupratphotos
Belmont Park: © Healy Racing
Churchill Downs: © Healy Racing

Del Mar: © Healy Racing
Gulfstream Park: © philipus / Alamy Stock Photo
Keeneland: © Healy Racing
Pimlico: © ZUMA Press, Inc. / Alamy Stock Photo
Santa Anita Park: © Healy Racing
Saratoga: © dupratphotos
San Isidro: © dupratphotos
Cidade Jardim: © dupratphotos
Gávea: © David Wall / Alamy Stock Photo
Santiago: © dupratphotos
Guayaquil: © dupratphotos
Monterrico: © dupratphotos
Montevideo: © Liz Price
Caracas: © dupratphotos
Ngong: © adrian arbib / Alamy Stock Photo
Champ de Mars: © Mo Peerbacus / Alamy Stock Photo
Casablanca-Anfa: © Casablanca Anfa - Mr Hicham Sbihi
Greyville: © Liesel King
Kenilworth: © Dan Abraham-focusonracing.com
Happy Valley: © Hugh Routledge
Sha Tin: © Healy Racing / © Ichiro Terashisma
Taipa: © Frank Sorge
Kolkata: © Paul Quayle / Alamy Stock Photo
Ooty: © Challiyan. Creative Commons CC0 1.0 Universal Public Domain Dedication.
Hanshin: © Ichiro Terashisma
Kyoto: © Ichiro Terashisma
Tokyo: © Ichiro Terashisma
Al Rayyan: © Dan Abraham-focusonracing.com
Riyadh: © Ali Zanadi
Taif: © Ian Cramman / Shutterstock.com
Kranji: © Peeo Ploff
Abu Dhabi: © Aladiyat/Akhalifa
Al Ain: © Ali Zanadi
Jebel Ali: © Aladiyat/Akhalifa
Meydan: © Aladiyat/Akhalifa / © Frank Sorge / © Aladiyat/Akhalifa
Birdsville: © Sharon Lee Chapman
Canterbury Park: © J Bar / licensed under the Creative Commons Attribution-Share Alike 3.0 Unported license
Caulfield: © Darren Tindale - The Image Is Everything
Dunkeld: © Mike Keating / Contributor Getty Images
Flemington: © Peeo Ploff / © Darren Tindale / © Sharon Lee Chapman
Moonee Valley: © Debbie Burt
Rosehill Gardens: © Sharon Lee Chapman
Royal Randwick: © Darren Tindale
Ellerslie: © Trish Dunell
Otaki: © Otaki racecourse
Trentham: © Michael McGimpsey / Alamy Stock Photo